D1593876

בס"ד

THE
Education Imperative

Guidance to Parents and Educators

From the Teachings of the
Lubavitcher Rebbe
Rabbi Menachem Mendel Schneerson זי"ע

Compiled, adapted and annotated by
Rabbi Nochem Kaplan

Merkos Chinuch Office

784 Eastern Parkway Suite 304
Brooklyn, NY 11213
www.chinuchoffice.org
office@chinuchoffice.org

ISBN 978-1-944875-20-6

Design and layout by Hasidic Archives
www.HasidicArchives.com
HasidicArchives@gmail.com

Cover art by Esty Raskin
Cover design by Design Is Yummy
Cover photo by Sholom Ber Goldstein

Printed in China

To my dear mother
Sarah Kaplan
of blessed memory

Contents

Principles in Education

Positive Focus   17
Empowering Children   24
Principles of Love   31
Charitable Education   35
Faith, Love, and Awe   40

The Parents' Role

The Influencers   49
By Example   55
Happy Home   61
Arising Challenges   67
Creating a Sanctuary   74
The Child's Space   81
The Responsible Parent   87
The Rock   96
The School Balance   101
Privilege to Support   107

The School's Role

Early Education 117

Storytelling 122

Teaching Self-discipline 127

Sacred Atmosphere 134

The Truth 138

Never Give Up 143

Fruitful Summers 147

Equal, but Separated 151

Additional Guidance 156

A Higher Education

The Beginnings of Sanctity 167

Instilling G-dly Awareness 172

The Personal G-d 179

Instilling Pride 185

Pride in Observance 193

Spiritual Development 199

Developing Torah Passion 204

Creating Immunity 210

The G-dly Relationship 219

The Letters 225

Future Focused 230

Twelve Essential Verses

Claim Your Inheritance   243

All from G-d   249

Get Past Your Past   255

G-d's Pride   261

It's Easy   267

Always There   273

The Master   279

Always Teaching   285

Keep Climbing   291

Service for Others   297

Creating Perfection   303

Feel the Joy   309

Stages of Education

In the Womb   317

Pregnancy   323

From the Youngest Age   328

Early Spirituality   334

Beginning of Formal Education   338

A Boy's Beginnings   343

Teen Idealism   347

Birthdays   355

INTRODUCTION

After his arrival on American shores in 1941, the Lubavitcher Rebbe, Rabbi Menachem M. Schneerson, was placed at the helm of several Chabad-Lubavitch educational institutions that had been founded by his father-in-law, the sixth Lubavitcher Rebbe, Rabbi Yosef Yitzchak Schneersohn.

The Rebbe quickly set about expanding them. While most Jewish leaders took a defensive stance when it came to teaching youth about a Torah-observant lifestyle, the Rebbe sought to help Jews develop a fierce pride in their Judaism. Instead of fearing difference, young Jews, he hoped, would embrace it as a unique identity. This became a hallmark of his activism that spanned decades of leadership. Torah-observant Jews should not be in retreat, the Rebbe taught, but be proactive in their outreach to the unaffiliated.

Under his leadership, as early as the 1940s, Jewish youth marched proudly along Brooklyn's Eastern Parkway, a turn-of-the-century boulevard inspired by the Champs-Élysées in Paris. They carried banners and placards extoling the holiness of Shabbat and the importance of Jewish education, often leaving an indelible impression on passersby.

In 1951, a year after the passing of his father-in-law, the Rebbe publicly assumed leadership of the Chabad-Lubavitch movement. Within a few years, his reputation had spread to such an extent that people came to Crown Heights in ever-growing numbers to seek his blessing and advice. Among them were Torah giants, American politicians, Israeli prime ministers, educators, and students.

During the Rebbe's forty years of dynamic leadership, Chabad became the largest Jewish educational organization in the world, impacting the lives of millions. The Rebbe's emissaries set up shop in Jewish communities around the world with his message of pride and activism.

These emissaries founded thousands of educational institutions, from preschools to adult-education programs. Today, there are hundreds of thousands of alumni of Chabad schools. They represent a cross-section of Jewish religious and social life, and, inspired by the Rebbe's approach, they are invariably proud of their Judaism. While the Rebbe was not directly involved in the curriculum or administration of any particular institution, countless schools and youth groups bear the imprint of his educational philosophy.

From his published works and letters, public talks, and numerous private conversations, we learn a great deal about the Rebbe's approach to education. However, little attempt has been made thus far to bring this wealth of material together in an organized fashion. Indeed, this is among the first efforts to make the Rebbe's teachings on education available to a broader public.

As in every other subject, the Rebbe looked to Torah to provide guidance about how best to educate the next generation. And just as he encouraged people to take pride in their Jewishness in other aspects of life, he sought to instill self-respect in the classroom and at home.

The word "education" may be understood as the formal process that takes place in a school setting, but the Rebbe saw education as encompassing all issues related to the rearing of children and their personal development. Children are impacted by all the adult behavior they observe. Thus, parents and teachers share responsibility for educating children, even if each has a distinct role.

Moreover, the Rebbe saw education as an ongoing process of self-refinement. Completing one's formal education does not mean that one should stop learning, growing, or improving.

The Rebbe spoke often about the spiritual dimension of a child's being and how home and school must nurture it cooperatively. When he spoke to educators, he pointed out their awesome responsibility in offering guidance on a broad range of topics. To parents, he stressed that raising children is a privilege; G-d gives them the opportunity to raise a new generation, and they have a responsibility to do so properly. Parents are to nourish and shelter their children, and also to create an environment in which their children may develop, morally and spiritually.

The Almighty does not require us to do the impossible, or to carry a burden too great for us, the Rebbe said. Thus, it follows that G-d endows parents with the ability to deal with any inherent challenges.

Daily, the Rebbe received hundreds of letters and requests for advice, opening each one personally. To most, he responded with a written comment on the letter itself, and to others he wrote a personal note. To date, dozens of volumes containing hundreds of letters have been published, representing only a portion of letters he authored.

His answers were invariably tailored to the needs and circumstances of the individual, and similar questions from different people were often answered in an entirely differently manner.

The Rebbe did not author a focused guide for educators and parents. This book does not present a digest of the Rebbe's thinking; rather, it is a compilation of what the Rebbe wrote and said. Since the Rebbe spoke in Yiddish and wrote in a number of languages (primarily Hebrew), this book is a free translation and adaptation. For the sake of coherency, the text was amended to follow a streamlined pronoun. In addition, to maintain the flow, we made efforts to condense duplicate concepts.

To provide context to the teachings, each chapter begins with a brief introduction to the subject matter at hand, followed by the Rebbe's actual words, with the sources identified in endnotes.

It is my hope and prayer that the lessons in this book will inspire parents and teachers to raise children proud of their heritage and devoted to passing it on to generations that follow.

Rabbi Nochem Kaplan

PART I

Principles
in Education

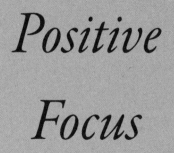

Positive

Focus

The basic psychology of Chasidism as taught by Rabbi Shneur Zalman of Liadi, 18th century founder of the Chabad movement and author of the *Tanya*, is that human nature is driven by rival influences. The corporeal being is comprised of a person's inclination toward self-indulgence, ego, personal desires, the *yetzer hara*, and an opposing inclination toward spiritual fulfillment and selflessness, the *yetzer tov*. This tug-of-war continues throughout life.

Education is the process by which children are taught what is right and what will help them develop into moral, compassionate human beings. Merely teaching dry concepts, or helping them learn by trial and error, may lead to a struggle for self-fulfillment through indulgence and personal gain, at the expense of what truly matters. Therefore, the greatest responsibility of a Torah educator is to imbue all subjects with lessons that children comprehend and that aim to refine their character.

More specifically, at all times, a Torah teacher must bear in mind the ultimate objective of the education process. The lessons need to provide both direct and subconscious messages so children can extract inherent moral and ethical cues.

Against this backdrop, we may understand the upcoming selections. The Rebbe cautioned teachers to concentrate less on what to avoid and not do, and more on what is appropriate and why it is desirable. He wanted the student to feel uplifted and inspired, not brow-beaten.

In a telling moment, the Rebbe encapsulated much of this. Following every festival, the Rebbe would distribute wine from his own goblet to the thousands who were present. He stood for hours as every individual passed by. He looked each person in the eye as he poured a small amount of wine into their cup. A newly-minted teacher passed the Rebbe and asked for a blessing as he embarked upon his career. Without missing a beat, the Rebbe said, "Build self-confidence."

The Rebbe wanted educators to imbue their students with an understanding of what is right so they would pay no heed to teasers or scoffers. He charged Jewish educators with the mission to develop and strengthen their students' spiritual inclination toward good, and imbue them with pride in their Jewish identity.

Character First

Education is not about the amount of knowledge a student will amass, but rather the development of positive character traits. This means that the student should strive to become the best version of themselves and behave good-naturedly in day-to-day life. This includes using their knowledge for righteous, honest, and peaceful purposes.

In other words, the student needs to first be shaped into a person with a moral character, while the acquisition of knowledge is secondary. When taught in this manner, the student will develop desirable traits that will then be apparent in their conduct.[1]

Beauty Centered

Students should be spoken to about the greatness of G-d, His creation, and the preciousness of the human being.

There should be more emphasis on the beauty of Judaism than on criticizing worldly materialism. That is to say, focus and dwell on bolstering positive behavior, and less on refraining from negative behaviors.[2]

No Shame

When educating youth, it is important to emphasize the opening of the Jewish code of law, "One should not be embarrassed by the people who scoff at one's service of G-d..." In addition, it should be emphasized that even if they don't grasp why mitzvahs are kept in a certain manner, the child follows the directives of their parents and teachers, who source their belief in Torah.[3]

Focus On Kindness

The fundamental and underlying obligation of each educator is to teach that G-d is the essence of goodness and kindness, and following this path leads us to a life of fulfillment.[4]

Teaching Kindness

To learn kindness, every student should have their own charity box and give charity, ideally every weekday morning.

Additionally, students should establish and run a loan society, wherein a child can donate their own money from time to time. The children should be encouraged to run it themselves, utilizing their time, energy and talents for a worthy cause. They should choose a manager and treasurer from among themselves, and rotate these positions among the students at regular intervals.

This will increase their sense of responsibility, connection – and inevitably, their enthusiasm – for an act of charity.[5]

1. *Torat Menachem 5742*, vol. 3, p. 1197.
2. *Sichot Kodesh 5728*, vol. 1, p. 506
3. Ibid, p. 506.

4. *Igrot Kodesh*, vol. 13, pp. 332-333.
5. *Likkutei Sichot*, vol. 16, p. 625.

Empowering

Children

One of the Rebbe's innovations was sending emissaries, *shluchim*, to do outreach in the farthest corners of the globe. The outreach mission of such an emissary is all-encompassing and becomes their life work. This mission is not merely a profession, for the emissary's family and home life are bound entirely with their goals. The couple must be a living example of what it means to be an involved Jew, and that extends to their children as well.

To help them achieve this goal, the Rebbe imbued his followers with a sense of duty and interpersonal responsibility. Thus, children of Chabad emissaries grow up as *shluchim*, and the Rebbe inspired and charged them with a sense of mission of their own.

While it is not easy to grow up different from most children, the drive these children demonstrate fortifies them with a unique sense of purpose. The Rebbe inspired the children of *shluchim* to reach out to their friends and become a catalyst for change amongst their peers.

The Rebbe wanted *every* child to become an emissary of G-d in their surroundings. This would give them the same advantage that children of *shluchim* have.

As mentioned earlier, the Rebbe was acutely aware

of the difficulties facing children who are different. He taught that children should take pride in their differences and use their friendships with other children to expose them to the world of Torah and mitzvahs. The Rebbe often said that while a child may feel that they are only drawing their friend closer to Torah, they are in fact strengthening their own connection.

Historically, children were viewed and portrayed as miniature adults, but this was not the Rebbe's approach. He wanted children to be children, but to have their Jewish pride propel them toward sharing their knowledge of the specialness of a Torah-centered life.

The Show Off

By nature, children typically want to show off to their friends. This natural inclination can be utilized for a holy purpose. Beyond learning at school, children can give their own Torah lessons based on what they've studied.

It says in Proverbs, "G-d's candle is the soul of a person" (20:27). Every person is like a candle that can kindle another flame, another soul. Thus, what the young "teach," should be in such a way that their "students" should be able to teach others in turn.[6]

Teaching Humility

Children should be guided to care for others, and not be dispassionate, haughty or disrespectful. By educating children to do acts of kindness, and give to the needy from their own money, which they could have used to buy something for themselves, the children are ingrained with attributes of humility and inclusion.[7]

Being Better

By nature, when children befriend others, they seek superiority in some way. This should be channeled for the good. Thus, when a child is playing with a friend, they have an opportunity to teach a Torah thought. And since competition is a powerful force, the second child, in turn, will teach the first child something they did not know.[8]

Channeling Energy

When a child has an overabundance of energy and acts wildly, there is no reason to be alarmed. On the contrary, their eagerness and energy should be channeled in a good direction, "good for the Heavens." In other words, into their relationship with the Almighty, into more enthusiasm for their Torah study, the fulfillment of mitzvahs, and the "good for His creatures,"[9] enabling them to do good with their peers.[10]

"How Could I?"

There is a well-known story about a great Chasid who had difficulty committing a sin, regardless of which one, because of his pride. He would say to himself, "Is it fitting for me, one of the great Chasidim of such a great Rebbe, to give in to the evil inclination, which would jeopardize my standing among the Jewish people and among the Chasidic community in particular?!" This is the way to influence a child: by elevating them with pride, and not berating them or making them feel less worthy.[11]

6. *Sefer HaSichot 5750*, vol. 2, p. 502.

7. *Likkutei Sichot*, vol. 16, p. 626.

8. *Sichot Kodesh 5736*, vol. 2, p. 146.

9. The Talmud, *Kiddushin* 40a.

10. *Torat Menachem 5745*, vol. 4, p. 2303.

11. *Igrot Kodesh*, vol. 8, p. 310.

Principles

of Love

Reading the Rebbe's talks and discourses, one easily reaches the conclusion that he saw the good within everyone and everything, that he believed love and encouragement to be the surest way to bring out the very best in children.

How can one use this approach in rearing children to have a strong moral backbone? How can one effectively teach discipline?

While the Rebbe never advocated a particular pedagogical approach, he instructed educators to keep a basic idea in mind: that one achieves more through love and encouragement than through enforcement of rules and regulations. This is as applicable to children as it is to adults. Children should be held to high standards of good behavior without the parents or educators needing to resort to fear or intimidation tactics. He was a proponent of non-confrontational disciplinary practices.

The Rebbe taught that positive behavior and character development should be taught and reinforced by elevating rather that suppressing a child. Thus, encouragement, reward and praise are helpful options when teaching desired behaviors.

Frightening Approach

One is more likely to leave a successful impact if they interact with a child pleasantly and peacefully. One should rarely use punishment, and if they do, they should ensure the child does not feel alienated.[12]

Through Reward

Since "all beginnings are difficult,"[13] new initiatives require more inner resolve. Therefore, when we begin to teach a child, we motivate them with rewards that are precious to them, as Maimonides taught,[14] "to accustom them to start out their studies."[15]

Specifically, the incentives should be ones that the child can appreciate at their present level, not items that may be relevant in the future.[16]

Holding Back

Chasidism teaches that the mind should rule the heart,[17] which means exercising restraint over feelings of the heart. While according to the Torah reprimands may be a valid way to educate a child, at the moment the educator witnesses an infraction, it is crucial that they control themselves and not react impulsively.[18]

Indirect Way

We are wired in a way that allows us to more readily receive instruction via non-confrontational encounters, therefore the adult should choose that method over one that is imposing commands or decrees.[19]

12. *Torat Menachem 5743*, vol. 1, p. 318.

13. Exodus 19:5, *Rashi*.

14. See Rambam's Commentary on *Sanhedrin*, beginning of chapter *Chelek*.

15. *Torat Menachem 5748*, vol. 2, p. 123.

16. *Igrot Kodesh*, vol. 21, p. 260.

17. Cf. *Tanya*, ch. 12.

18. *Igrot Kodesh*, vol. 11, pp. 135-136.

19. Ibid, vol. 18, p. 296.

Charitable

Education

The Rebbe went out of his way to teach children to give charity. Frequently upon arriving at Chabad headquarters and upon leaving, he would distribute dimes to the children in his path and instruct them to put the coins into a charity box, the *pushkah*. When he spoke at children's gatherings, he invariably had teachers distribute his dimes. He instructed children to give charity at every special occasion. Clearly, he wanted children to make charity a habit.

In the few selections that follow, we read that teaching children to give of themselves and their possessions is a cardinal principle. They must learn that they are messengers of the Almighty in helping those who are less fortunate.

To Give Of Oneself

It is important to educate the child to forgo their natural instinct of keeping everything they own for themselves and instead to give of their own money to someone whom they owe nothing. This nurtures the sense that they are not in this world simply for their own self-regard, a trait that is the source of much adolescent angst.[20]

As it is common practice to give pocket money to children, they should be taught to give a portion of it, be it a few pennies, nickels or dimes, to their charity box.[21]

Without Question

A child should grow up with the knowledge that their home is a charitable one. This means that beyond donating ten or even twenty percent of one's earnings, when they find someone in need, they do not wait to be asked. Rather, they give immediately and without restraint.[22]

A child, even from a young age, should be educated to give charity. Even if it is not their money, when they grow older, they will continue to give as they did when they were young.[23]

Personal Box

Each child should have a personal charity box and be given coins to donate every weekday.[24]

In addition, a charity box should be affixed to the wall permanently, so that the entire room should become a charitable room.[25]

Tasking a School Principal

So that students should learn to donate from their personal savings, the principals should give money – even a coin – to the students, teachers, and school employees, from personal funds or the institution, to be given to charity. This should be done at least once a week and preferably before Shabbat when the needs of the poor are greater.[26]

20. *Lekutei Sichot*, vol. 36, p. 267.

21. *Sefer Hasichot 5750*, vol. 2, p. 485.

22. *Torat Menachem*, vol. 24, p. 276.

23. *Torat Menachem 5743*, vol. 4, p. 2033.

24. *Teshuvoit Ubeurim*, p. 312.

25. *Torat Menachem 5748*, vol. 4, p. 346.

26. *Sefer Hasichot 5750*, vol. 1, p. 108.

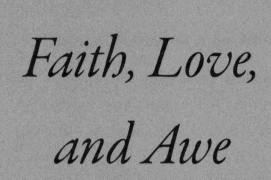

Faith, Love, and Awe

How to instill belief in the Almighty is a question that has occupied religious educators for generations. How does childish innocence become mature faith? Regardless of one's personal perspective, it is clearly a process that begins in childhood. So how best to start?

The Rebbe stressed that the bedrock of a religious education is to teach children to accept instruction and be guided in advance what is expected of them.

For this to work, the Rebbe explained, parents and teachers need to continually earn and maintain their children's trust. For children to become convinced that something *my teacher told me*, or *my mother said*, is without a doubt so, adults must always tell children the truth.

The Rebbe's teachings about the fundamentals of education are predicated upon this basic premise.

Constant Recognition

If a parent continually indulges a child, they will begin to believe that they are entitled to everything, even what belongs to another. In this way, they will come to fulfill our sages' definition of an immoral person who says, "What's mine is mine, and what's yours is mine."[27]

Fear of authority may deter the child from acting on this impulse for a time, but it is not a solution, for they will simply steal when no one is looking.

The path to avoiding such conduct is to inculcate the child with the recognition that there is "an eye that sees, an ear that hears, and all your actions are recorded in a book."[28] At the same time, one should be introduced to the Torah concept of *teshuvah*, returning to the proper course. We are not immediately punished when we err, for, in loving-kindness, G-d provides us the opportunity to return.[29]

The Creator

The true, firm foundation of education is the knowledge that, as our sages have taught, "There is a Master of the universe."[30] G-d the Creator conducts the world, supervising every detail. This knowledge influences a person to behave appropriately.[31]

A Moment of Providence

Children should be taught that G-d "performs great wonders and miracles,"[32] and arranges all the details of the world in order to fulfill their basic needs. They should be taught this, not only because it is the correct approach to education, but because it is the truth.

Rabbi Israel Baal Shem Tov, founder of the Chasidic movement, once sent the great Torah scholar Rabbi Chaim Rappaport to a certain location where he should drink from a particular spring. Afterwards, Rabbi Israel told him that this particular spring had been waiting since Creation for him to recite a blessing on its water.[33]

Similarly, when a child is walking on the street and becomes thirsty, and, at that moment, a truck passes by selling kosher drinks, the child should know that it is not a coincidence.

Rather, it is Divine providence, with the Almighty orchestrating that the person selling the beverages should wake at a certain time and drive their truck out at certain time, so that the two would meet at a precise moment. G-d orchestrates all this so the child will be satiated and have a clear mind to study Torah. And the truth is that the street corner where the child made the blessing has waited since Creation for that particular child to bless G-d in that particular spot.

A child who is given this kind of education will relate to the world in an entirely different manner. [34]

27. *Ethics of Our Fathers* 5:10.

28. Ibid 2:1.

29. *Torat Menachem 5743*, vol. 3, p. 1342.

30. *Breishit Rabah*, beginning of ch. 39.

31. *Torat Menachem 5743*, vol. 2, p. 899.

32. Psalms 136:4.

33. *Likkutei Dibburim,* vol. 4, 596a ff.

34. *Sichot Kodesh 5741*, vol. 1, pp. 245-247.

PART II

The Parents' Role

The

Influencers

n his talks and writings, the Rebbe often said that parents frequently do not fully appreciate the power of their influence, nor do they know how to harness their authority.

When I asked for his advice on behalf of distraught parents, he told me: "Tell them they are parents, and since the Almighty does not expect the impossible from them, He will also grant them the wisdom to deal with this."

The Rebbe encouraged positivity. He told parents to make their children – especially those experiencing difficulty – feel special, and build their self-esteem.

As we shall see in the excerpts below, he counseled parents to never withdraw or despair. The Rebbe believed that parents give up too often, or feel inadequate when meeting resistance; instead, they should wisely choose what they say and how they say it and not become despondent from the child's backlash. Additionally, the Rebbe counseled parents to engage their children's friends and peers to exert their influence.

It is important to note that sometimes we see the Rebbe's approach clearly, but at other times, clarity is elusive. In addition to the ideas culled in previous chapters, the passages that follow are not meant to present a clearly-articulated or resolute position on the subjects they address. Rather, they are a collection of personal responses that may be just as relevant today as they were decades ago. How to apply the Rebbe's advice is left to each individual.

Many of these responses are to parents who sought greater influence on their children and were seeking the Rebbe's advice on doing so successfully. Some of the Rebbe's advice is of a practical nature and some has a spiritual connotation.

The Parents' Influence

Parents should value the influence they can have over their children. When they make efforts in this area, they will surely have a great impact. In any case, even if their impact does not effect complete change, they will certainly have a great degree of influence.[35]

Difficult Solution

When seeing difficulties with their children's behavior, parents should examine how much time they spend with their family, including their spouse.[36]

Never Tire

Bitterness does not help a child return to the correct path. A parent needs to involve themselves in the situation, of course via pleasant means. Despite the difficulty, one should not tire of speaking about the issue, once, twice, or three times, until it reaches the child.[37]

G-d's Envoys

Educating one's children is G-d's commandment, and since G-d, the Father of all of us, practices what He commands,[38] He educates children through the parents. Parents are thus envoys on behalf of G-d in schooling their children. And with that in mind, what the sages say, "one who toils and succeeds is believed,"[39] is much easier to attain.[40]

Deeper Strengths

When there are difficulties or challenges, it is a test that G-d has given us. G-d wants us to dig deeper for greater, hidden strengths that we possess. In the face of the challenge of raising a child, all that is necessary is strong willpower.[41]

35. *Igrot Kodesh,* vol. 4, p. 344.

36. *Petakim*, vol. 6, p. 161.

37. *Igrot Kodesh*, vol. 5, p. 80.

38. The Midrash, *Shemot Rabbbah* 30:9.

39. The Talmud, *Megilllah* 6b.

40. *Petakim*, vol. 1, p. 186.

41. *Igrot Kodesh*, vol. 18, p. 53.

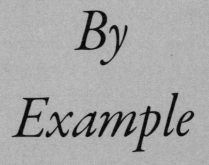

By

Example

The child-rearing role granted by the Almighty, the Rebbe postulates, is not just a physical one but also a spiritual responsibility. In fact, when considering the entirety of a child's education, as opposed to meeting the child's fleeting material needs, it is the spiritual dimension that has lasting value.

The idea that parents have a proprietary role vis-à-vis their children is erroneous; rather, parents have a Divinely-mandated responsibility to provide for their children. The spiritual dimension of this role is paramount.

The Rebbe once told me that being a truly "good" parent challenges one to the core and requires a great deal of effort. The Rebbe further explained that the Almighty does not burden us with anything we cannot discharge and grants parents the ability to meet their responsibilities.

With that, the Rebbe stressed that we ought not expect an immediate positive response to every step we take. Education is a long, cumulative process and every investment therein has a beneficial effect. Only time may tell how a child learns and grows because of what we teach and demonstrate. The Rebbe often encouraged parents and educators not to seek immediate results but to keep investing in children.

Parents do not own their children.

G-d gave them children for safekeeping, to raise and educate appropriately.[42]

The Partnership

The sages state that there are three partners in the creation of a person: father, mother, and the Almighty.[43] Providing for the education of the child – the most precious deposit possible – is the job of the parents, while material needs – food, livelihood, health, and the like – is the responsibility of the Almighty.[44]

Wholehearted Example

To successfully influence children in their Jewish practice and identity, one should strengthen their own commitment to Judaism. Thus, when children see their parents wholeheartedly conduct their lives in this way, there is hope that the children will accept their parents' requests in this regard.[45]

The Sapling

Education can be compared to caring for a delicate seed or sapling. Every additional act of nurturing and care brings about results that are of indelible impact once the seed or sapling becomes a fruit-bearing tree. And so, too, in the reverse, G-d forbid.[46]

The Investment

The same way men are obligated to don *tefillin* daily, the Rebbe Rayatz said, parents are required to contemplate their children's education for a half-hour every day.[47]

The concept behind *tefillin* is the dedication of one's intellect and emotions to the Almighty.[48] Therefore, it is used here as a metaphor, for one should invest in their child's education so that they will dedicate their minds and hearts to G-d.[49]

42. *Torat Menachem 5744*, vol. 1, p. 504.
43. The Talmud, *Kiddushin* 30b.
44. *Torat Menachem 5743*, vol. 3, p. 1482.
45. *Igrot Kodesh*, vol. 8, p. 19.
46. Ibid, vol. 26, p. 59.
47. *Hayom Yom,* 22 *Teves.* Cf. *Igrot Kodesh Admor Harayatz*, vol. 13, p. 47.
48. *Shulchan Aruch, Orach Chaim,* 25:5. *Shulchan Aruch Harav, Orach Chaim,* 25:11.

Happy

Home

In many of his talks and writings, the Rebbe discussed the importance of the family unit and the Jewish home. He saw it as the foundation of Jewish life, and its integrity as pivotal to raising the next generation. The Rebbe charged both parents with the responsibility of maintaining a harmonious atmosphere within the home, explaining that synchronized efforts are needed if they are to succeed.

The issue of harmony in the home is discussed in the earliest Talmudic sources, dating back millennia. The Rebbe stressed the importance of couples seeing the best in each other and learning to overlook weaknesses. He encouraged compromise and cooperation in purposeful unanimity, thereby creating a home that is a happy place for children.

Much attention was focused on what is referred to as "the generation gap," or the disparate attitudes of people from different generations. Such a "gap" leads to lack of understanding, resulting in a younger generation that doesn't appreciate their seniors and an older generation that complains about the youth. The Rebbe explained that this issue stems from not passing on a clear value system to the next generation, resulting in poor communication between them.

Harmony at home helps bridge that gap, and the younger generation is the beneficiary; it helps them develop their own strengths and appreciation for their parents.

In addition, he explained, the home is a microcosm of Jewish society and impacts the entire Jewish people. The Rebbe's philosophy often concentrated on the individual unit because the world is comprised of many, many small units. A harmonious Jewish home impacts the children and their friends; from there, it spreads from the individual unit into the world at large.

Offshoots of Harmony

Harmony in the home is a central, critical and lofty ideal, especially when a couple is blessed with children. The importance of children growing up in a home where there is peace, with both parents present, is obvious. Clearly, if it is necessary to compromise, even on important matters, it should be done for the good of the children.

In addition, compromise should be made happily and whole-heartedly, without feelings of self-sacrifice, duress and so forth. On the contrary, they should feel they are doing something good for their home and children's welfare.[50]

Mirror Effect

A child's education begins with the connection and unity of the family through daily observance of Torah, especially those that families observe together, such as Shabbat and holidays.

When parents do all they can to strengthen the family unit, being aware of the happenings in their children's lives, during the week and especially on Shabbat and holidays, they are in a position to give their children genuine guidance. When children are enveloped in authentic love and awe, they will happily accept guidance offered by a parent.[51]

Generational Unification

An essential part of education is teaching peace, unity, care for another and instilling belief in a Creator that runs the world. Proper education brings closeness and unity between the younger person (the one being educated) and the older person (the educator), and between children and parents, thus minimizing the gap. Together, multiple generations can act as one unit, utilizing each of their G-d-given talents for the good of the entire family. In fact, emphasizing education through love is more successful than creating a culture of fear.[52]

49. *Sichot Kodesh 5740*, vol. 3, p. 217.

50. *Nitzutzei Or*, p. 98.

51. *Likkutei Sichot*, vol. 12, p. 209.

52. *Torat Menachem 5750*, vol. 3, p. 194.

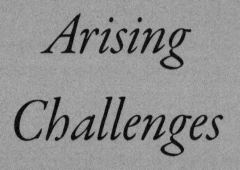

Arising

Challenges

O ver the years, parents would ask the Rebbe how to deal with a variety of parenting issues. Below, in addition to previous selections, is a selection of his answers.

Reading his guidance, one discerns the Rebbe's belief that even children who exhibit difficult behavior can be managed. He expected parents to get professional help where it was warranted, but even then the parents themselves were to be involved in the process.

Through his working day, the Rebbe was engaged in global matters and counselled leaders from the broadest spectrum of Jewish communal life. Despite this, though, he paid attention to the personal and even the mundane affairs of ordinary people. One might assume that someone of his stature would delegate such things to subordinates, but the Rebbe remained engaged with the problems of daily life and offered his personal attention to any individual. For many, just having the Rebbe respond to them was motivation and encouragement enough; this alone gave them the energy to deal with the problems they faced.

Complaints Guided

When a child complains about their teacher or counselor, they should be guided with stories that teach how a negative situation turns out for the good. The stories should include people who recognize that what seemed bad at first was in fact so good that they gave thanks to G-d.[53]

Seek Advice

In dealing with extremely mischievous behavior, one should consult with experienced educators.[54]

Using Medications

When it is difficult for a child to be under supervision all day and follow a set schedule, they should be given the minimum dosage of behavioral medication necessary and be regularly monitored by a doctor.[55]

Via Friends

Children are often less inclined to accept advice, guidance or suggestions from parents because they feel their parents still consider them immature or wish to impose authority, etc. Experience show that it is more effective to influence a child via friends or acquaintances rather than directly from the parents.[56]

Among other reasons, unlike parents or close family who may not always muster self-control, friends can have influence without becoming overly emotional.[57]

The friend should speak to them about the matter, even multiple times, with words that emanate from the heart. With that, it should not be obvious that the friend is acting as the parent's agent.[58]

Need of Motivation

When a child is not motivated, it is a good idea, in addition to their regular studies, to give them a leadership position in a group activity, such as directing a group of younger children. This will add to their independence and their joy in daily life.[59]

Strong Friends

When a child shows signs of being aggressive, the parents should find them friends who are equally as strong and thus able to check the child's actions.[60]

Positive Change

When we look at a child's actions positively, and express it with words, this automatically has an effect on them, and their actions will improve accordingly.[61]

Even when parents are sure that they are one-hundred percent correct, it is unwise to follow each of their child's moves and try to direct their conduct.[62]

Leaving Home

When living at a distance from proper Jewish education, and a choice must be made for a spouse to move near the school with the child or for the child to be there alone, the latter is preferable. For children to live away from home is a common practice, while it not natural for spouses to live apart. Of course, the child should be placed in the care of a trustworthy family.[63]

Strengthening Qualities

When a child cannot learn how to read and write, one should consult with a medical specialist. The discussion should also include how to nurture the areas that the child has already developed, as this will encourage improvement in the areas that need strengthening.[64]

53. *Torat Menachem 5745*, vol. 4, p. 2303.
54. *Igrot Kodesh*, vol. 20, p. 296.
55. Ibid, vol. 17, p. 287.
56. Letter from April 17, 1972.
57. *Igrot Kodesh*, vol. 15, p. 88.
58. Ibid, vol. 24, p. 201.
59. Ibid, vol. 19, p. 373.
60. *Petakim*, vol.1, p.197.
61. *Igrot Kodesh*, vol. 16, p. 49.
62. Ibid, vol. 28, p. 82.
63. Ibid, vol. 10, p. 229.

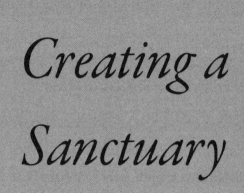

Creating a
Sanctuary

The Jewish home as a place of sanctity – where the atmosphere is palpably different from the popular culture outside it – was a theme the Rebbe often addressed at Chasidic gatherings, in his writings and during private audiences.

The Hebrew word for sanctity, *kedushah*, is used by the Torah and in rabbinic literature to reference separation from the mundane. Both "sanctity" and "separation" are relevant to understanding the Rebbe's teachings. A Jewish home must be a place where spirituality is an objective, a means to elevating everyday living and infusing meaning into it. A Jewish home must be a place that children understand is qualitatively different.

The first prerequisite is harmony, for strife and unhappiness create an environment that prevents sanctity from developing. In addition, the home should be a place where spiritual values are absorbed by children because their parents exemplify those values. What better way to teach the value of Torah study than for children to see a parent spending time in study? How can children better learn the value of honesty than by observing their parents' honest interpersonal relationships?

The *kedushah* values that permeate a home are not achieved without determination and devotion; they are the product of hard work on the part of parents.

The Rebbe talked a great deal about electronic media to which a child is exposed. Parents may do all they can to infuse their home with meaning and moral purpose, but they have no control over what a child is exposed to by outside sources. Decisions as to what is suitable for children are made by producers of such media who may have a completely different set of values, often diametrically opposed to Torah values. Those type of influences should not be welcome in our homes.

The Rebbe did not advocate separation from society but he also warned against adopting all of its cultural norms and values. We need to be within society but we need not be of it; we may indeed need to adapt modern technology, science and cultural ideas to our Torah life, but only to better lead a life of *kedushah*.

Pride Saves

When Reuben went out during the time of the wheat harvest and found jasmine flowers in the field (Genesis 30:14), the famed Biblical commentator Rashi states, "It was the time of the harvest, yet he did not stretch out his hand to steal, to take wheat or barley," which were readily available, "but only to take an ownerless thing, which no one cares about." It could be deduced from Rashi that his behavior was unique and others did not conduct themselves this way.

Down to the detail of the flower species Reuben found, the Torah is describing that the tribes understood that their conduct should be different, commensurate with Torah values in every respect.

We learn from this that one need not follow the spirit of the times. From a young age, a child should know that their home is different. Even when exposed to influences encouraging them to act wrongly, a child leans into the knowledge that they are different and need not follow negative influences.[65]

The Home Spirit

When it comes to Torah study, a child should experience a sense of awe and passion that this is Divine wisdom.

The child should feel that their parents are charitable and generous. If someone is in need, there is no delay in assisting them, even beyond the prescribed amount of 10 or 20 percent.

The child should know that the parent may remain in synagogue after the prayer services conclude, not only to pray with a quorum of 10, but to spend time in the service of G-d via contemplative prayer.[66]

Seeing Violence

Television is responsible for an unparalleled breach of standards. Even non-Jews have come out with campaigns against television, which is devastating for children.

We can see the effect that viewing violence had in the case of four Jewish teenagers [who were involved in several murders and acts of violence in 1954], and other similar cases of murder. Everyone admits that one of the causes of this phenomenon is television and movies, where killings and shooting are the norm.

Moreover, even if one thinks they will only watch "pious" programs on television, how can parents guarantee that children will not view other forbidden programs as well? The children will argue that if the parents view television, they may also view whatever they like.[67]

Productive Music

One needs to distance themselves entirely from music that encourages people to act on forbidden desires and indulge every fad. This includes music that is not only secular, but calls on the listener to turn to their beastly inclinations and encourages the destruction of limitations, order, modesty, etc.[68]

Torah Saturation

Though the child spends most of their day in school, coming home to eat and sleep, they should sense an appreciation for Torah in the home. This is created when a parent uses every free moment to study Torah, when holy books are in use around the home, and Torah concepts and ideas are highlighted in conversation.[69]

64. Ibid, vol. 16, p. 3.

65. *Likkutei Sichot*, vol. 3, pp. 792.

66. *Torat Menachem*, vol. 24, p. 276.

67. *Likkutei Sichot,* vol. 18, pp. 459-461.

68. Ibid, vol. 38, p. 179.

69. *Shaarei Chinuch*, p. 127.

The
Child's Space

There was a time, not so long ago, when children were considered lucky to have their own bed in a shared bedroom. We have progressed significantly in this regard, and thus need to pay attention to the messages that a child's home surroundings convey.

The Rebbe called for homes to be replete with holy books, meant to be studied from. The same, the Rebbe argued, is true of children's rooms. Parents should help their children create an environment dedicated not just to welfare and comfort, but to spiritual development as well.

The imaginary separation we often create between a child's physical needs and their moral and spiritual needs suggests that the two are independent of one another when, in fact, they are actually intertwined. The Rebbe asserted that attempts to develop a strong sense of ethics without belief in the Almighty at its foundation will lead to moral relativism and a set of values subject to change.

Thus, the Rebbe encouraged creating a spiritual environment in a child's private space and filling it with objects that have religious purpose. Ultimately, the objective of creating an environment conducive to spiritual development is to ensure that a child's behavior reflects the contents of the holy books in their personal space.

When children learn to be respectful of their rooms, they also learn that that they can bring holiness into their environment simply by their behavior.

Just as children learn that certain behaviors are not acceptable in public or sacred places, they also learn that their rooms are special spaces where some refinement is encouraged.

Holy Impression

A bedroom contains a bed, desk, etc. The focus, however, should be on filling the room with holy books, so that ultimately each and every item in the room is dedicated to Torah. In fact, the very presence of books makes a strong impression.

At the very least, there should be a *Chumash* (the Pentateuch), a *siddur* (prayer book), and the Passover *Haggadah.* It would also be a good idea to have a *Tehillim* (Psalms).[70] In addition, there should be a charity box.

When these are visible, it will remind the child of Torah and its mitzvahs. It will also encourage a visiting friend – who may be unaware of such things – to inquire as to their purpose. The host will respond that with a *siddur* one prays to the Almighty, from the *Chumash* one learns the Torah of G-d, and with a charity box one fulfills the great mitzvah of giving to the poor. This may inspire a friend to do the same in their own room.[71]

Their Temple

Even the youngest child needs to ensure their home is pure and holy like the Holy Temple itself, and that there is a King directing their daily activities.[72]

Their Domain

The child is the "judge" and "officer" over their own personal conduct and room, which includes ensuring that everything is in its proper place and the books are clean and available when needed for study.[73]

Daily Visual

In their books, children should inscribe the verse
from Psalms (24:1): "The world and everything within
it belongs to G-d." The child will see it each time they
open a book and remember that the whole world
belongs to the Creator. Underneath, the child should
write their Jewish name, indicating that they devote
themselves to G-d.[74]

72. *To the Sons and Daughters of Our People
Israel, Everywhere*, vol. 2, p. 498.

70. *Torat Menachem 5747*, vol. 2, p. 648.

71. *Torat Menachem 5748*, vol. 4, p. 346.

73. *Torat Menachem 5749*, vol. 4, p. 215.

The

Responsible

Parent

The Rebbe continually spoke of parental responsibility toward children. He spoke of the meaning of the word education and its spiritual connotations and of the great efforts required of parents to extend themselves beyond their perceived limitations.

One of the Rebbe's frequent expressions was *mesirut nefesh*, self-sacrifice, which he also used in reference to parenting. The concept of *mesirut nefesh* can easily be misinterpreted and taken literally. What it means in this context is that parents need to extend themselves to their very limit in order to help children maximize their spiritual potential.

Parents should set aside their own needs for the sake of their children; the Rebbe thought that this was a requisite mindset. He spoke of normal parental desires to see children excel and outdo them, but he stressed that this is equally applicable to their children's spiritual growth and development.

In his talks, the Rebbe would often analyze a Torah passage and draw lessons related to a point he was making. We read a number of these lessons in the selections that follow, presented here in brief.

Sacrificing for Every Jewish child

In the Biblical story of Joseph in Egypt, and Judah's confrontation with him in which he begs for the release of their brother Benjamin, the verse states, "And Judah approached him" (Genesis 44:18). The sages say that when he approached Joseph, he was prepared for any eventuality, even to wage war. [75]

Why then did Judah endanger himself to such an extent for Benjamin? The verse states, "For your servant has pledged to be a guarantor for the child" (Genesis 44:32). Jacob's other children were alive and well, but because Judah claimed responsibility for his brother, he was prepared to sacrifice himself.

This is a lesson for every parent. G-d has entrusted them with children, and each parent must be prepared to display self-sacrifice for each child. [76]

Parents' Educational Commitment

Our sages tells us that at the Giving of the Torah, the Jewish nation proclaimed that their children would be guarantors that the Torah would be observed.[77] In other words, the Jewish people told G-d: "Take note of the education we give our children, and then You will see that the Torah can be entrusted to us."

It is natural that what a person was lacking, or missed in their youth, they desire to provide for their children. We cannot comprehend a person's actions because, perhaps, their evil inclination is too strong for them to overcome. However, when it comes to the education of their children, a good parent does not spare any effort or money. In fact, when it comes to their children's education, a parent is able to overcome any negative inclination so that the children will not repeat their own errors.

Thus, we told G-d at Mount Sinai that one can discern a person's level of commitment from the way they educate their children. We need to remember, however, that it is easy enough to make excuses to ourselves. But we cannot fool our children. When we decide that there is a part of Judaism we prefer over others, the children will follow suit.[78]

Children First

When discussing the process of life, the sages use the phrase, "children, life, and livelihood."[79] One would think that the correct order is first life, followed by livelihood, marriage and children.

When pondering this, we can conclude that life is not life, and livelihood is not livelihood, until we have children. This is why our forefather Abraham, who was blessed with wealth and fame but was childless most of his life, said of himself, "I am but dust and ashes."[80] Without children, his life was bereft.

In fact, the first commandment of the Torah is to have children, and only then "I am G-d, your G-d," stressing the great importance of children and the dedication required of us.[81]

One Entity

When our forefather Abraham sent Eliezer to find a wife for his son Isaac, the famed commentator Rashi tells us that Abraham wrote a deed that entrusted Isaac with everything he owned. He did this in order to assure that the prospective bride's family would not hesitate to send their daughter.[82]

Isaac was a grown man at the time, over 37 years of age. He was able to "stand on his own two feet," was established religiously and had even passed the greatest test of all at the Binding of Isaac. Still, Abraham gave all his belongings to Isaac to ensure a suitable bride, leaving nothing for himself.

From this we learn that parents must be devoted entirely to their children and experience the bond between them as a singular unit. One needs to be prepared to give up everything and remain wholly devoted to the child's upbringing.

This is true, too, for the teacher, whose students are akin to his own children. They must make every effort – to the point of self-sacrifice – for the education of their pupils.[83]

The Bond

When Hannah brought her son, Samuel, to the Holy Sanctuary in Shiloh, she said, "For this child I prayed, and He granted my request... And I have also lent him to the Almighty, all the days of his life" (Samuel I:27-8).

One popular interpretation of this phrase is: "I am presenting my son 'on loan,' like a person who lends a vessel to their teacher."[84] According to this, Hannah only lent Samuel to the Almighty, but her connection to him remained constant. He was still hers. This speaks to the everlasting bond that must exist between a mother and her son, between parents and their children.[85]

From Infancy

The circumstances surrounding our forefather Isaac's birth were supernatural and miraculous. His circumcision took place when he was eight days old, and his upbringing was fraught with difficulties.

Quite different was the case of Abraham's older son Ishmael, whose early upbringing was quite normal, and who was circumcised at a mature age, when he was thirteen years old.

Yet it was Isaac whom G-d chose to be Abraham's true heir, and from whom the Jewish people would descend.

Thus, the Torah teaches us that when new generations are to be born – which ensure Jewish continuity – the approach must not be based on natural considerations and human calculations. For Jewish existence is not dependent upon natural forces but upon G-d's direct intervention and Divine providence.

Similarly, the education and upbringing of Jewish children is not to be determined by the considerations and criteria of the secular world. Jewish parents do not wait until a child is mature enough to determine his own behavior and path to Judaism. They are given the strongest and fullest possible measures of Jewish training from infancy.

Only in this way is it possible to ensure that their Jewish education – and the "everlasting covenant" with G-d – withstand all difficulties with strength and be endowed with G-d's blessings, materially and spiritually.[86]

74. *Likkutei Sichot*, vol. 14, pp. 279-280.

75. The Midrash, *Bereshit Rabbah* 93:6.

76. *Likkutei Sichot*, vol. 1, p. 94.

77. *Shir HaShirim Rabbah* 1:4.

78. *Torah Menachem*, vol. 66, pp. 279 and 281.

79. The Talmud, *Moed Katan* 28a.

80. Genesis 18:27.

81. *Sichot Kodesh 5737*, p. 630.

82. Genesis 24:10, *Rashi. Bereshit Rabbah* 16:59.

83. *Sichot Kodesh 5730*, vol. 1, p. 209.

84. Cf. *Rashi*.

85. *Torat Menachem 5744*, vol. 1, p. 158.

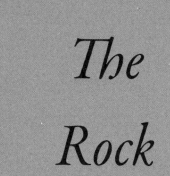

The

Rock

The Rebbe often reflected on the gentler, nurturing nature of a mother. Through the love she shows her children, he said, a mother is better able to help them develop their love for Jewish ideals.

The Rebbe explained that the Torah assigns a unique role for women. It is not just a matter of religious requirement, but because the Almighty has unique expectations from each gender.

Without disparagement toward women with careers, he stressed that the primary role of a mother involves educating her children. The Rebbe encouraged women, saying it is their good fortune to invest their G-d-given gifts into raising the next generation of dedicated Jews.

Parent of Identity

Jewish identity is determined via the mother. If she is Jewish, the child is Jewish. From this we can extrapolate that raising a Jewish child is the merit and under the care of the mother.[87]

Via Love

King Solomon says, "The wisdom of a woman builds her home" (Proverbs 14:1), for she wisely guides through love and affection, in contrast to the father who may resort to harsher enforcement tactics. This is why the sages referred to her as the embodiment of the home, for she is the central giver in the home, especially in regard to infants.[88]

Necessary Traits

A child's development during their early years is dependent on the mother, for she exemplifies the three attributes in which the Jewish people excel: compassion, humility, and generosity – which are all of utmost importance for education.[89]

The Vanguard

When G-d gave the Torah, He first turned to the women,[90] for when the environment and the "street" are not saturated with Judaism, and at times society is in opposition with Torah, it is the woman that remains a vanguard of Jewish life.[91]

Kind Rebuke

By nature, women are gentler, displaying closeness, love and affection, more so than men. Therefore, rebuke given by a mother is more effective.[92]

86. Letter from November 2, 1969.

87. *Torat Menachem*, vol. 56, p. 198.

88. *Torat Menachem 5748*, vol. 4, p. 341.

89. *Sefer Hasichot 5752* vol. 2, p. 357.

90. *Rashi* on Exodus 19:3, from *Mechilta*.

91. *Igrot Kodesh*, vol. 23, p. 184.

The School

Balance

Too often, there is dissonance between parents and the school system. Parents may feel that a school is not dealing with their child appropriately, while the school is of the belief that parents have unrealistic expectations. This type of escalating exchange can cause the parent-teacher relationship to deteriorate.

At times, when parents face a problem, they seek to place blame on outside sources and have difficulty facing the fact that it is their responsibility to solve it. Invariably, the Rebbe advised parents that while they are indeed responsible for their child's education, they need to view the school as an ally and work cooperatively with their child's teachers.

School as an Agent

While schools have a responsibility to educate, the primary responsibility falls on the parents. When children see that their education is central to their parents' lives, and the school serves as an agent on behalf of the parents, it becomes easier to guide their actions at school.[93]

Inherent Biases

Often parents are biased when it comes to their children. Because of this blind spot, they may be predisposed to lenience or excessive strictness. Therefore, it is best to actively consult with those who know the child and the issue at hand,[94] or the school administration.[95]

With Joy

The first time we take a child to school, we do so happily. In fact, this is the way it should be done daily. [96]

School Qualms

A parent should take an interest in the way their children are educated. When it is not clear why the school took specific action, the parent should ask questions and make suggestions. However, this does not make them the school's director. When there are issues that need to be resolved, for the sake of the students, they should be reconciled without tumult or dispute.[97]

When the challenges necessitate a change in schools, it is best to wait until the new school year.[98]

Challenges at School

There are two ways to approach challenges at school. One is to weigh the pros and cons and decide what to do. The second is to consider what it would take to tackle the difficulties with determination and resoluteness – an approach that will teach new ways to overcome challenges. The latter is preferable.[99]

Seeking to Rectify

When there is difficulty at school, it is easy to run from the issue, saying, "As long as I am safe, I don't care." However, it should be the parent's privilege and duty to foster change that will benefit all the students. As our sages say, even if a person has tried 99 times to make a change, they should try again.[100]

Sure Place

When parents communicate to a child that they are unsure if the child should remain at a school, is it difficult for the child to make the challenging situation work. When the parents are certain that the child will be at the school, the child will make it work.[101]

92. *Torat Menachem 5746*, vol. 3, p. 617.

93. *Torat Menachem 5744*, vol. 3, p. 1434.

94. *Igrot Kodesh*, vol. 20, p. 284.

95. *Igeret Hachinuch*, p. 235.

96. *Torat Menachem*, vol. 16, pp. 328-329.

97. *Heichal Menachem*, vol. 1, pp. 126-127.

98. *The Letter and the Spirit*, vol. 3, p. 86.

99. Ibid, vol. 3, p. 87.

100. Ibid, p. 147.

101. *Igrot Kodesh*, vol. 17, p. 287.

Privilege to Support

P rivate religious schools often receive minimal governmental funding. Thus, funding for Jewish day schools has always been a serious concern to the community.[102]

Too often, Jewish communities settle for second best when Jewish education is involved: poorly trained teachers, weak curricula, low expectations, and fewer hours of instruction. If education is relegated to second best, the Jewish community suffers immeasurably. The children are indifferent to what they learn since they see it carries low priority to their parents. The Rebbe spoke of this incessantly.

He encouraged philanthropists to fund Jewish education but also expected individuals to understand its importance and dig into their pockets. He frequently advised parents to strive for the very best when it came to the religious education of their children.

The Rebbe told parents that education is the Almighty's priority, and it must be theirs. If they do what is incumbent upon them, they can expect reciprocity from G-d.

Education of the child is the responsibility of the parents, and thus it is worthwhile for them to dedicate at least part of their charitable giving to a local educational institution.[103]

G-d's Deposit

When it comes to a child's education, parents should not be satisfied with the mediocre, but strive for the very best possible. If this is true regarding matters related to physical health, it applies all the more to spiritual matters related to the child's soul, which is "truly a part of G-d above."[104]

Even if the best education comes at great expense, it is not a reason to attempt to save money, for the money that goes toward education is given to parents as a "deposit" from G-d to be used for educating their children in the path of Torah and mitzvahs.

As our sages said: There are three partners in the creation of a person – father, mother and G-d. [105] The partnership is divided so that providing for the spiritual needs of a child is the parents' domain. This means that the Almighty entrusted them with a child, the most precious deposit possible, in the hope that they will fulfill their role in ensuring their child's soul is nourished.

In contrast, the material needs of a child – food, basic needs, health, and the like – are G-d's responsibility. When parents uphold their responsibilities in the partnership, then G-d, as well, fulfills His portion of the partnership.[106]

First Portion

From one's income, parents should first set aside the sum needed to pay for the Jewish education of their children. Household expenses should only be taken from the remainder of one's income.[107]

The Expense

G-d runs the world, sustains it and grants our needs. Therefore, it is not possible that acting in accordance with G-d's directive, by giving one's children a Torah education, will have an adverse effect on one's livelihood.

On the contrary, when we strengthen ourselves and act in accordance with the will of the Creator, even though it may come with difficulties, we merit the fulfillment of G-d's promise, "If you act in accordance with My statutes," which our sages interpret to mean toiling in Torah, for learning Torah comes through great efforts,[108] "then the land will give forth produce" (Leviticus 26:3-4). G-d will give us livelihood in even greater measure.[109]

---

102. School choice and other such programs have emerged, but during the Rebbe's lifetime most of these options did not yet exist.

103. *Torat Menachem 5747*, vol. 2, p. 649 and 651.

104. *Tanya* ch. 2, beg.

105. The Talmud, *Kiddushin* 30b.

106. *Torat Menachem 5743*, vol. 3, pp. 1482-1483.

107. *Torat Menachem*, vol. 19, p. 194.

108. *Rashi* on the verse.

109. *Igrot Kodesh*, vol. 9, p. 174.

PART III

The School's Role

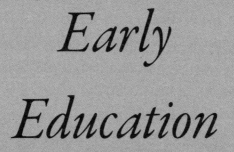

Early

Education

I n a letter I once received, the Rebbe explained the idea of "meaningful education." He noted that all instruction of children must take into account the long-term effects upon them. This applies, he wrote, to each subject and how it is presented. He made clear that it is not singularly about what educators teach, but about what children learn and how they will integrate it into their lives.

Chasidic thought draws a distinction between the written word and an engraving, applying it metaphorically to various situations. The written word is external to the paper upon which it is written; the engraving, however, becomes one with the material upon which it is pressed. The Rebbe used this metaphor to demonstrate how the educational process can have a lasting impact.

This is especially important when considering early childhood education. Small children are like sponges, absorbing whatever they are taught. This applies both to formal instruction and to what they learn by osmosis. Everything they experience makes a difference.

Therefore, if educators and parents are to impact a child's spiritual development, they should practice careful forethought to what and how they teach.

Preschool

It is a good idea to have a child attend preschool, not so much as a matter of developing learning skills, but to aid their conduct and nurture positive behavior.[110]

Long Lasting

Especially with regard to children, the general rule is that for any concept or information to be absorbed and have lasting benefit, it must relate and connect with an actual experience or with tangible expression in the child's life. Thus, it can be expected that knowledge, coupled with an experience, will have a lasting effect outside the school walls.[111]

Hold the Rebuke

With young children, one should embrace them and offer them rewards. With stern rebuke, an educator can completely distance a student.[112]

Second Nature

A very young child cannot comprehend the meaning of mitzvahs. Therefore, the child's education should be "engraved," and fulfillment of mitzvahs should become part of their nature and habit. For example, when a child wakes from their sleep, they instinctively recite the *Modeh Ani*.[113]

Learning Texts

When a child turns three, they should be taught from Jewish texts, in addition to what they are taught orally.[114]

110. *Igrot Kodesh*, vol. 14, pp. 39-40.

111. Letter from September 12, 1973.

112. *Likkutei Sichot*, vol. 17, p. 74.

113. *Sefer Hasichot 5749*, vol. 2, pp. 472-473.

114. *Igrot Kodesh*, vol. 12, p. 288.

Storytelling

A story serves to best illustrate a difficult concept and is ultimately more impactful than intellectual discourse. Chasidic educators often use stories to both interest and engage their students and in hope of leaving a lasting impression.

Some have objected to storytelling at the expense of text-based learning, but experience has demonstrated the value of engaging a child emotionally through stories. The Rebbe weighed in on the side of storytellers. He cautioned, however, that not every story serves the purpose of Jewish education, no matter how interesting it may be.

Furthermore, the Rebbe postulated that children should be exposed to miraculous stories as a tool to develop a strong bond with the Jewish faith. The Torah and vast body of rabbinic literature are replete with wonderful stories. Jewish lore is also full of stories of the righteous, *tsaddikim*, and their miracles, but these are not fairy tales; rather, they are a documentation of the Almighty's presence.

Some have argued that fantastical tales may help a child develop their curiosity and creativity, but the Rebbe cautioned against this approach, specifically advising parents not to tell children "tall tales" and to never lie to them.

The Story Advantage

A child may be wary of learning material that seems beyond his grasp; they may fear that they will not understand it. However, when a lesson is communicated in the form of an illustration, the child may better comprehend the idea and take it to heart. In addition, stories arouse a child's interest so that they want to hear more and more.[115]

On Self-Sacrifice

Even children should be taught the Torah about how Abraham attempted to offer his son as a sacrifice to G-d (and the like), because by nature a child feels and understands the concept of self-sacrifice, often relating to it even more than adults.[116]

Passionate Truth

The stories told to children should not be fables, but rather sourced from the Torah or true stories about our sages.[117] Telling them such stories with enthusiasm and passion will bring it "alive" in the child's mind, often leaving a lifelong impression.[118]

The Miraculous

In order to instill faith and the understanding that happenings around us are beyond our grasp, children should be told of supernatural, miraculous events.[119]

115. *Torat Menachem 5745*, vol. 4, pp. 2302-2303.

116. *Torat Menachem 5749*, vol. 1, p. 349.

117. *Sichot Kodesh 5741*, vol. 1, p. 246.

118. *Torat Menachem 5746*, vol. 3, p. 394.

119. *Likkutei Sichot*, vol. 19, p. 92.

Teaching
Self-discipline

While the Rebbe understood the need for discipline, he suggested that self-regulation is ideal. He said numerous times that the greatest weakness of American Jewish youth is that they question the very idea of Divine authority, *kabbalat ol*, and find difficulty in following any guidelines.

The Rebbe saw *kabbalat ol* as the foundation of Jewish life and successful education. Children should not be free to challenge their teachers regarding why they need to learn one thing or another. They should learn to appreciate the dictates of their parents and teachers and accept the fact that their elders generally know what is in their best interest.

Educators and, broadly speaking, all adults within a child's sphere of influence should have high expectations, use personal encouragement, and utilize positive measures as much as possible. Any reprimand, the Rebbe said, must be accompanied by actions that can positively influence a child's behavior in the long-term. Additionally, he expected adults to help children practice self-discipline, but not to create a controlled or frightening environment where children cannot be themselves.

The Middle Ground

In the United States, many psychologists support indulging children. Since it is necessary to work with a professional, it is necessary to consider their opinions. With that – especially since some have already disagreed with this approach – one should explain to them that there is a middle-of-the-road approach.[120]

The Foundation

It is commonly acknowledged that discipline is the foundation for success in learning and conduct.[121] The goal of education is to lay foundations that the child can refer to for the rest of his life. When a child is taught about righteousness, honesty, Torah and mitzvahs, and the Thirteen Principles of Faith, they should understand: "This Torah will not be changed."[122] Then, when they have a desire for something negative, they can refer back to their unwavering foundation.[123]

Focus on Positive

One should refrain from lengthy descriptions of evil. Rather one's main focus should be the virtue of true goodness. The best way to accomplish this is through informal gatherings on topics appropriate to the children's level of understanding, and include storytelling, singing, dancing, and so on.[124]

Mealtime

Mealtimes can foster emotional closeness, so they should be utilized to instill manners in accordance with Jewish customs and observances. [125]

Hitting

Hitting a child is more destructive than productive. Other methods – like temporary suspension, expulsion, or preventing the child from participating in certain activities – might also be employed, but the best option is to increase supervision over the students. This should minimize undesirable behaviors until they stop altogether.[126]

Not Just the Classroom

A good educator cares not only for their students' acquisition of information. They also teach their students to be refined in conduct: eating, sleeping and behaving appropriately outside their immediate environment.[127]

Embrace the Right

It is necessary to protect a child from negative influences. When pointing out undesirable influences, the reproach should be, as the sages say, "[the] left hand rebuffs."[128] They metaphorically emphasized that rebuke should be done with the less dominant "hand" and not with the same force as the measure used for "the right" and stronger hand, which should be used to embrace them.[129]

PART III   The School's Role

120. *Igrot Kodesh*, vol. 19, p. 298.

121. Ibid, vol. 10, p. 86.

122. Ninth of Maimonides' "Thirteen Principles of Faith."

123. *Torat Menachem 5744*, vol. 1, p. 105.

124. *Igrot Kodesh*, vol. 12, p. 378.

125. *Igrot Kodesh*, vol. 14, p. 409.

126. Ibid, vol. 21, p. 195.

127. *Sichot Kodesh 5736*, vol. 2, p. 149

128. The Talmud, *Sanhedrin* 107b.

129. *Igrot Melech*, vol. 2, pp. 143-144.

Sacred

Atmosphere

While the Rebbe did not want to separate from the world at large, when it came to early education, he advocated for the creation of an environment free of all detrimental influences.

The Rebbe encouraged parents and educators to occupy children with positive activities, so that they won't find themselves with the free time to get involved in things that might ultimately impact them negatively.

The Schedule

It is clear that in education there must be order and a firm schedule.[130] When a student has too much free time at their disposal, doing with it what they wish, our sages[131] advised: "Free time leads to boredom, and boredom leads to sin."[132] Therefore, efforts should be made to schedule their day to capacity.[133]

Cleanliness

When a person neglects their physical appearance, dress and hygiene, it reflects on their internal state.[134] Similarly, physical cleanliness facilitates a vessel for spirituality, which then invites additional holiness (*kedushah*) and purity (*taharah*) into the soul.[135]

Joyous Times

When a child is joyous, the evil inclination makes every effort to turn the joy into unruly conduct. A child may then lose self-control and refuse to listen to instructions. Therefore, one should give a child outlets to express their joy regarding mitzvahs, such as on Jewish holidays.[136]

130. *Igrot Kodesh*, vol. 9, p. 274.

131. The Talmud, *Kesubos* 50b.

132. *Igrot Kodesh*, vol. 14, p. 148.

133. Ibid, p. 43.

134. *Sefer Hamaamarim Kuntreisim*, vol. 2, p. 322b.

135. *Likkutei Sichot,* vol. 32, p. 68.

136. *Torat Menachem 5744,* vol. 1, pp. 269-270.

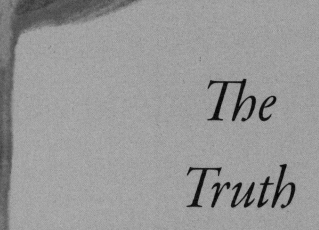

The

Truth

The Rebbe was scrupulously honest and expected those around him to maintain the highest degree of personal integrity, too. He expected this of educators as well. As mentioned earlier, when it came to children, the Rebbe taught us to look beyond the here and now, and to consider long-term effects. What subliminal message are we sending? Will children be impacted positively by what they see and hear from us?

The Rebbe expected adults to model behaviors they wanted their children to learn. He repeatedly said that parents and teachers must be a *dugma chaya,* a "living example," of what they expect from their charges. The idea of "do as I do" – and *not* "do as I say, not as I do" – must be a hallmark for all those who have influence on children.

Truth from Truth

Some believe that it is permissible to interpret sacred text untruthfully, with the intention of explaining it accurately when the child matures. However, when one implants the opposite of truth, truth cannot possibly sprout from it. Truth only grows from truth![137]

Promises

When one promises a reward to a child, it must be fulfilled. One should be especially careful with young children, since with older children there may be reason not to follow through at times.[138] When a child is promised something and the promise is not kept, they lose trust in his caregiver, for they see dishonesty.[139]

The Lie

Even when we have the best of intentions, we should be very careful not to tell children falsehoods. Being untruthful will leave the impression that lying is permissible, and there is no way to know how the evil inclination will take advantage of this.[140]

Contradictions

In order to instill the foundations of Torah within children, their teachers need to behave in accordance with it. One cannot fool a child.

When an adult's conduct contradicts what they teach, the child asks, "Why do my parents expect that Torah matters should be 'like new'[141] for me while they do the absolute minimum to fulfill their own obligations?"

They may even harbor these thoughts and feelings for years until they verbalize it. When an adult acts in opposition of Torah, this devalues what their children are taught, and causes the child to lose trust in the parent or teacher.[142]

137. *Sichot Kodesh 5739*, vol. 1, pp. 609-610.

138. Cf. The Talmud, *Yevamos* 65b.

139. *Sichot Kodesh 5736*, vol. 2, p. 278.

140. *Torat Menachem 5744*, vol. 2, p. 1248. Cf. *Torat Menachem 5748*, vol. 3, p. 307,

fn. 8.

141. *Rashi* on Exodus 19:1, 11:13, and Deuteronomy 26:16.

142. *Torat Menachem 5744*, vol. 3, p. 1534; and ibid, vol. 1, pp. 113-114.

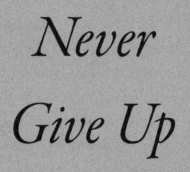

Never

Give Up

At times, a student can be problematic, and faculty may wish that they enroll elsewhere. The Rebbe, however, wanted schools to do their utmost to assist students with any issue.

The Rebbe advised that, generally speaking, since the many take precedence over the needs of a single individual, expulsion might be considered if a student is influencing others detrimentally. However, the Rebbe believed that there are few students who are so incorrigible that they cannot not be reached or better influenced. He wanted teachers to see their students' potential, not always as great students, but as people who possessed Divine gifts and a G-d-given life mission.

Once, upon learning that I had expelled a student from school, I received a call from the Rebbe's aide instructing me to find an alternative placement for the student. At times, expulsion may be justified as a last resort, he said, but the school is still responsible for the student's education and welfare, and cannot abdicate that responsibility. Interestingly, my subsequent relationship as a mentor to this student endured many years.

Negative Influencers

When students are having an undesirable influence over their friends, there are no rules that are applicable to all, since ever person varies profoundly from another. Therefore, the teachers who know the students best should be consulted, weigh the pros and cons, and then act accordingly. While the good of the majority takes precedence, nevertheless some approaches can be tried:

Oftentimes, increasing supervision of those students quickly improves their conduct and their influence over others.

When a student is given a position of responsibility, they feel the need to set an example. Many times, this invites improvement in their spiritual growth, good conduct, etc.[143]

Keep Close

When students are pushing the limits of school rules, one must do everything in their power so that not even a single student is abandoned. Through positive guidance, good friends and Chasidic gatherings, change in their conduct is anticipated.[144]

When effort is made, most often the conduct of the student changes. First, they will stop being destructive towards others, and afterwards they'll correct themselves.[145]

General Good

The communal good takes precedence over the benefit of an individual, therefore not every student who wants to be accepted needs to be accepted. This especially applies when a potential student was expelled from other schools because of poor behavior.[146]

143. *Heichal Menachem*, vol. 1, p. 125.

144. *Igrot Kodesh*, vol. 10 page 173.

145. Ibid, vol. 7, p. 310.

146. Ibid, vol. 14, p. 302.

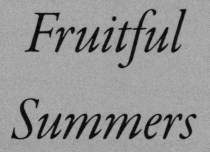

Fruitful

Summers

The Rebbe taught that time should be spent wisely not just during school hours or on homework and the like; time should be thoughtfully utilized even during summer vacations.

While the venue, variety and intensity of learning may need to change during summer, he said, children should not be allowed to waste their vacations. The very idea that a child should feel no sense of responsibility during the summer was foreign to him. Of course, the heat of summer may demand a different setting and a child should be given more time to relax and enjoy physical activity that the school year might not allow, but the Rebbe believed that schools cannot abandon their students during the summer.

The Rebbe frequently spoke of making good use of the summer. He advocated sleep-away summer camps so that children could be immersed in a Jewish atmosphere, enjoy experiences and develop skills that they would otherwise not acquire.

The concerns were not limited to students in lower grades; he spoke vehemently about yeshivahs remaining open for students throughout the summer.

Keeping Occupied

A child should not have time that is completely "empty of substance," even on summer days. Although children are not in school, there are ways to create huge impact. Potential activities include telling meaningful stories, or role-play games where a child can be taught about charity or helping others. One such game of searching for a "treasure" can emphasizes how each child searches for the "treasure" hidden within the world and in each person.[147]

Clear Schedule

Because students have a break from secular studies, during "vacation days" it is easier to ingrain matters of Torah and Jewish observance.[148]

School Continues

Even during vacation, a school should never close its doors. It should remain open for students to come and study. If teachers feel it is necessary for health or other reasons to take a break during school break, it should be coordinated and staggered in a way that will allow the school to remain open.[149]

147. *Torat Menachem 5746*, vol. 3, p. 618.

148. *Likkutei Sichot*, vol. 23, p. 407.

149. *Igrot Kodesh*, vol. 11, p. 293.

Equal, but
Separated

Co-education is now the norm and any variation from it – at school or worship, at work or play – is considered discriminatory. The Rebbe rejected the idea of co-education; equality does not mean sharing everything, he held.

The Rebbe saw opposition to co-education as not only a religious imperative, but a moral one. He believed that education suffers when students are distracted and that natural attraction leads young people to behaviors that are morally objectionable.

The upheaval of moral values, which are basic to religious behavior, have alarmingly begun to affect youth at an increasingly younger age. One need only browse media and advertisements aimed at children and young adults to see how pervasive this has become. The Rebbe saw the direction in which this social revolution was heading and, many decades ago, voiced his opposition in the strongest of terms.

His stance against co-education was met with antagonism even from some religious circles, but the Rebbe remained steadfast and continued to encourage educators to separate the genders whenever possible. With that, he wanted girls to have the same opportunities as boys, while making it clear that gender roles differ.

At All Costs

The purpose of education is to raise a child religiously, morally and ethically to the utmost possible degree of perfection. Co-education is *not* conducive to the attainment of this end; on the contrary, it is a sure step in the opposite direction. The moral state of present-day youth is too painful a subject to dwell upon. Many educators outside the religious school system have also come to realize the harmful effects of co-education.

This is relevant from the youngest age, for the habits of a young boy or girl becomes their nature in the following years, and so on. Needless to say, the financial argument that it is more expensive to run separate classes for boys and girls is no argument at all, since the matter vitally concerns the future of many children. And even if the future of a single child was involved, money is of no consideration. As our sages say,[150] "He who saves one life is deemed to have saved a whole world."[151]

Academic Progress

Separation of genders in the classroom is not merely a question of religion, but, as is known, also an ethical and even an educational one. A student's attention may be distracted from their studies and the school labs, impinging on their academic progress.[152]

Increase the Student Body

When there is opposition toward separating genders in small schools, efforts should be made to increase the student body. There will then be need for a new teacher, or at least an assistant teacher, and there will be a worthy opportunity to divide the classes accordingly.[153]

Assemblies

It is worthwhile to make one assembly for boys and girls at the same time, in order to not draw attention to the separation. This should be done in a way that ensures separation in the assembly hall itself. If there is doubt, especially in regard to singing, then there should be two assemblies.[154]

Entrances

It is preferable that the school be built with separate entrances for boys and girls. If possible, they should be housed in separate buildings and streets. The greater the caution in such matters, the more praiseworthy it is.[155]

PART III The School's Role

150. The Talmud, *Sanhedrin* 37a.
151. *Letters from the Rebbe*, vol. 2, p. 44.
152. *Igrot Kodesh*, vol. 17, p. 29.
153. Ibid, vol. 16, p. 284.
154. Ibid, vol. 19, p. 261.
155. Ibid, vol. 6, p. 33.

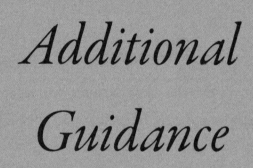

Additional

Guidance

The Rebbe did not see the education process as limited to school hours; a school needs to care for their students 24/7. Nor should a school assume that parents are on the same page or have interest and/or the wherewithal to augment what a child learns in school. It was the school's responsibility, the Rebbe suggested, to develop rapport with parents and help them understand and reinforce the school's objectives for their child.

The Rebbe told school principals that while children may graduate and move on, they should remain life-long students of their teachers. He instructed schools to maintain contact with their alumni, not for financial support or other interests, but to help alumni in their continued spiritual development.

School curricula, the Rebbe taught, must be tailored to the long-term needs of students – what is commonly referred to as "affective education."

In addition to specific guidance discussed in previous chapters, here are some additional ideas posited by the Rebbe.

Hands-on Projects

When a student does not come from a Torah-observant home, the curriculum should be adapted to allot more time for the practical aspects of Judaism. They should be provided hands-on teaching about the weekly Torah reading and Shabbat in general, such as candle-lighting, *kiddush*, and the like. This also applies to special days on the Jewish calendar, particularly festivals.[156]

Rewards

While it is good for a competition to raffle prizes (as the sages state, "Competition between scholars increases wisdom"[157]), Torah books and the like should also be incentivized.[158]

Educational Beginnings

Early education should not begin with intellectual explanations, but rather with faith in and acceptance of G-d. Even mitzvahs that can be understood intellectually should be done because "it is what G-d wants." Thus, we tell young children miracle stories that defy explanation, implanting within them belief in G-d.

The Rebbe Rayatz, Rabbi Yosef Yitzchak, once hired a teacher for his children who did not subscribe to this approach. In the teacher's worldview, biblical stories of miracles were to be left to mature students who have already grasped intellectual concepts. As soon as the children's grandfather, the Rebbe Rashab, Rabbi Sholom Dovber, learned of this, the teacher was dismissed.[159]

Specifically Youth

One could argue that the teacher in the previous story had a point. After all, we are enjoined to "educate the lad according to their way" (Proverbs 6:22). This, Maimonides explains at length, means to teach with material incentives, until the child chooses to study for the sake of Heaven, without reward.[160]

Teaching only what can be grasped at the child's level of maturity may work well for academic subjects, but belief in G-d is applicable to all ages, and G-d's infinity needs to be conveyed from the beginning. Clothing the miraculous in the vestments of natural order is not just partial belief. It is not belief at all.

Beginning with miracle stories ensures that when the child matures intellectually, there will be no weakening of their faith in the supernatural, because a strong foundation has already been laid.

Educating a child "according to their way" means imbedding strong belief so that "even in old age," when one's intellect has matured, they "will not swerve from it."[161]

The Influence

Positive influence can be not only through an educator's guidance, but and even more so through their conduct.[162] This includes mode of dress, not only for teachers of higher grades, but also the lower ones.[163]

Oversight

An institution bears responsibility for the individual and the group. Therefore, institutions should designate a committee of three, who are *not* part of management, to examine whether the institution is growing and fulfilling its duty.

While they should encourage and insist on change, it should be done in a respectful and pleasant manner. In fact, the more they probe, the more the administration will feel an obligation to accomplish.[164]

Parental Connection

It is important to establish an ongoing relationship with parents, including meeting with them from time to time. This way, parents can be encouraged to extend the school's environment at home, and share values of Torah education. This will encourage parents and school staff to discuss issues, explore resolutions, and address obstacles that may exist between children and parents.[165]

Beginning and End

At the beginning and end of a lesson, one should say a maxim about practical mitzvah observance or a thought that speaks to the reverence of G-d. [166]

Gender Matters

For greater impact and influence, girls should be taught by female teachers.[167]

The Alumni Connection

Keeping in touch with former students will in many ways have a positive effect on them.[168] Connection with alumni should be handled with the same enthusiasm as if in the classroom. With that, the relationship should be developed according to the maturity level and knowledge base of the students. [169]

156. Letter from September 12, 1973.

157. The Talmud, *Baba Batra* 21b.

158. *Shaarei Chinuch*, p. 238; Answer from April 8, 1983.

159. *Likkutei Sichot,* vol. 19, pp. 91-92.

160. On the Mishnah in *Sanhedrin*, beginning of the chapter *Chelek*.

161. *Torat Menachem*, vol. 29, p. 310.

162. *Igrot Kodesh*, vol. 13, p. 352.

163. *Shaarei Chinuch*, p. 284.

164. *Sefer Hasichot 5748*, vol. 2, p. 597.

165. *Likkutei Sichot*, p. 398.

166. *Igrot Kodesh*, vol. 15, p.132.

167. *Sichot Kodesh 5728*, vol. 1, p. 506.

168. *Igrot Kodesh,* vol. 7, p. 324.

169. *Torat Menachem 5749*, vol. 3, p. 207.

PART IV

A Higher
Education

The

Beginnings

of Sanctity

P arents are partners with the Almighty in bringing children into the world and raising them. While G-d provides the body and soul, it is the parents' responsibility to impart values that guide their children to lead a refined and G-d-centered life.

G-d does, however, offer guidance. The Torah makes it clear that education is not primarily concerned with attaining a physical livelihood, but with crafting a purposeful and spiritually meaningful life. With the Torah as a guide, children learn to channel their natural gifts, talents, and inclinations to find spiritual satisfaction as well as material success.

Children naturally seek to satisfy their needs and desires. Left to their own devices, they may grow up self-absorbed and egocentric. But a Torah-centered education connects them to a less selfish dimension, where they can adhere to G-d's will and the concept of a Higher Authority. This type of education – which Jewish literature calls *chinuch* – begins very early in life.

In his talks on education, the Rebbe uses the word *kedushah*, literally "holiness," which implies sanctification of the mundane by infusing it with spiritual purpose. Sanctifying the world is humanity's ultimate mission, and this idea should be a very concrete part of a child's education. In the early stages, it is represented in dual objectives:

1. Teaching children about their relationship with G-d.

2. Teaching them that their interactions with others are also of Divine concern. We do not hurt others, not only because we don't want them to hurt us, but because this very idea is rooted in the fact that we are all G-d's creations, and He wants us to treat everyone with sensitivity. We thus sanctify our own behavior by infusing it with spiritual purpose.

Similarly, the concept of *yirat Shamayim*, reverence for the Almighty, does not imply fear of an omnipotent Being, but the idea that G-d cares about me and my behavior. Thus, G-d is introduced as a loving, caring Father who brought us into existence in order to lead lives of good deeds and self-improvement.

In this way, children are raised with a sense of endearment to the Creator, and with the understanding that by trying to do the right thing, they connect their lives with Divine purpose. At first, they experience this in an infantile way, but as they grow, their sense of connection to G-d matures.

Ultimate Education

The purpose of education is to help a child become accustomed to the idea of sanctification, which connects their soul with G-d.[170] Such education is built upon an awareness of the Almighty's omnipresence and a sense of awe, as the verse states, "The beginning of wisdom is the awe of G-d" (Psalms 111:10), in addition to feelings of love and closeness to G-d. It is upon these foundations that Jewish observance is built.[171]

Changing Habits

The Torah informs us, "The natural inclination of man's heart is bad from his youth" (Genesis 8:21). It is natural to be self-absorbed. The Torah charges us to educate a child and an adult to direct this natural inclination so that the mind dominates and regulates the heart. The objective is to strive toward a loftier, less self-absorbed, and more G-d-centered life. [172]

Parental Responsibility

Every child is a child of G-d; their parents were given the merit of birthing them, and the responsibility to raise and educate them. This task includes conveying values, teaching morality, and connecting a child's soul to the Divine Presence. In other words, parents ought to inculcate their children with the desire and means to fulfill G-d's will.[173]

The true purpose of education is not only to acquire knowledge but also to instill a yearning for holiness. This objective is reached by habituating children to a life dedicated to G-d's will as taught in the Torah.[174]

170. *Likkutei Sichot*, vol. 35, p. 12.

171. *Torat Menachem 5749*, vol. 3, p. 75.

172. *Sefer Hasichot 5747*, vol. 1, p. 74.

173. *Torat Menachem 5747*, vol. 2, p. 650.

174. *Likkutei Sichot*, vol. 35, p. 12.

Instilling

G-dly

Awareness

The ultimate objective of a Jewish education as it is presented here is to instill the eternal truths of the Torah. It does not address social or academic development, but the development of morality as taught by the Torah, so that children can build their lives with core beliefs and faith at their fulcrum.

To achieve this, the Rebbe taught that we must engage children on issues of faith. We need to explain our beliefs to them, but, more importantly, we need to act upon our beliefs.

Why do bad things happen to good people? G-d is omnipresent, but He is not obvious. The nature of G-dliness is concealed. If all our deeds were immediately rewarded, if good people had all they needed and bad people suffered, there would be no free choice. The world could not exist as He willed it. Children, said the Rebbe, need to hear this.

Regarding *yirat Shamayim*, literally "fear of Heaven," the stress should not be upon the fear, but rather on Heaven. What it really means is that we wish to recognize the omnipresence of the Almighty, to have reverence for G-d, and that we do not *want* to act in a manner contrary to His wishes. Helping children experience this, on their level, is what education is all about.

Lessons are sometimes overt, but more often covert. Children will observe a parent or teacher act in a particular manner and draw their own conclusions. Many daily manifestations of religion are an expression of our *yirat Shamayim*, such as wearing a head covering, ritual washing of our hands, and prayer. It's not just a matter of training children to the point where ritual becomes habit, but emphasizing the inner meaning of the act.

G-dly Enthusiasm

A child should be educated to have a deep yearning for G-d. The center of their world should be Torah, and what the "world" says should not matter. This way, when a child visibly experiences G-d in their daily life, the child will brighten their surroundings with G-dliness.[175]

Long-Term Effect

Rebuke should always be administered with kindness. This does not mean, however, that in the name of being amiable, one should concede in matters relating to Jewish observance or reverence for G-d. This is doubly true when it comes to education, when any change in standard may affect an entire class of students who will soon be building Jewish homes.[176]

Privileged Responsibility

Every single Jew, and particularly every child, is precious to the Almighty, even more than an only child is to their parents. Therefore, surely the Almighty wants to grant each child blessings and success in all matters.

Those who educate them, however, have a responsibility and privilege to do everything in their power to ensure their students are vessels to receive G-d's blessings. This includes helping children become accustomed to wearing a *kippah* and *tallit katan* [ritual fringes]; taking care to recite the *Modeh Ani* prayer with them upon rising, morning blessings, blessings on food, the *Shema,* and the like. When educators do all the above, they will succeed in their mission.[177]

Connected Family

Family members are connected to each other not only genetically but also spiritually. When one family member increases their G-dly reverence, it affects the others. This is especially so regarding the parents' behavior and its impact upon the children; as positivity increases in the home, the children will feel it and respond.[178]

A Lifetime of Belief

It takes a lifetime to internalize the idea of G-d's unity, and this process should begin in childhood.

When teaching a child the *Shema Yisrael* prayer, "Hear O Israel . . . G-d is One," use the exemplum of kings. You should explain that there are kings; then there are kings of kings; and then there is the King over all kings. Even a young child will understand that there is no equivalent to G-d.

As the child grows older, this explanation is no longer sufficient. In addition to G-d being the King of all kings, explain that there is no sovereignty except G-d, and everything in existence is like an axe in the hand of a lumberjack, which has no freedom in choosing what to chop. In fact, in this regard, the unity of G-d is greater, since the axe itself exists at this moment because of G-d. In due course, when the child matures even more, explain that there is no existence outside of G-d.[179]

175. *Likkutei Sichot*, vol. 15, p. 134.
176. *Igrot Kodesh*, vol. 17, p. 109.
177. Ibid, vol. 5, p. 330.
178. Ibid, vol. 23, p. 376
179. *Torat Menachem 5714*, vol. 12, p. 148.

The

Personal

G-d

We are reluctant to talk to children about complex ideas that are beyond their ability to understand. We don't have simple language to convey such ideas, and, naturally, children lack the intellectual development to understand. We'll only confuse them, we conclude.

The Rebbe felt that we need to find simple terminology to impress upon children the basic tenets of faith. The stages of Divine unity, discussed above, help children associate G-d with a childlike concept of greatness that captures their imagination. Waiting for them to mature before introducing the idea of G-dliness is counterproductive.

According to Jewish thought, every creature in existence was created for a purpose. The Psalmist speaks about G-d "counting and naming every star," and so it is with all creation.

When a child understands that G-d cares for and sustains all His creatures, the conclusion is clear: "I am important and everything that I encounter is there to help and guide me." Simultaneously, they must know that G-d cares about their actions and behavior.

These ideas are difficult even for adults to live by, so children should hear them early and often.

In the following selections, the Rebbe discusses how to teach children about Divine purpose and guidance. He does not shy away from telling children that G-d performs miracles; on the contrary, he wants children to internalize the idea that G-d's relationship with us is not limited to what we expect or understand.

Morality and Belief

When G-d gave the Torah at Mount Sinai, the children were made guarantors to ensure that the Jewish nation would keep the mitzvahs. The Ten Commandments begin by instructing the Jewish people to believe in G-d and not worship other deities – only then come the more direct commandments against murdering, stealing, or coveting. The lesson is that education must be based upon belief in G-d's existence and rejection of anything that denies it.

Unfortunately, this truth was put to the test in the recent past: the Germans, who championed progressive philosophies and ideals, held no reverence or awareness of G-d, and ultimately sank into the basest barbarity. Torah, however, which is "a teaching of life,"[180] guarantees not only eternal life in the World to Come, but also a moral life in our world.[181]

Self-centered

Young children naturally feel that everything in their environment was created for them. In fact, the Talmudic adage relates that every person should say, "It is for my sake that the world was created."[182] However, children should be educated to channel these feelings in the appropriate way and recognize that they have a unique part in making the material world a home for G-d.[183]

PART IV — *A Higher Education*

Beyond Calculation

Children should be taught that, as part of an ancient nation that has experienced thousands of years of trials and challenges, our survival is dependent on miracles. Since our very existence is beyond human calculation, from a young age they should be encouraged to set aside worry regarding their future livelihood.[184]

180. *Amidah* liturgy.
181. *Igrot Kodesh*, vol. 22, p. 236.
182. The Talmud, *Sanhedrin* 37a.
183. *Torat Menachem 5750*, vol. 2, pp. 131 and 139.
184. *Torat Menachem 5718*, vol. 21, p. 159.

184 The Education Imperative

Instilling

Pride

As parents raise children, they instill a set of core values. Sometimes this is intentional but oftentimes children learn vicariously. These values teach them what is important and what is not, which behaviors are acceptable and which are not. Parents, directly and implicitly, instruct their children how to interact socially, and how to have personal integrity.

Too often, however, parental guidance about spiritual matters is lacking, despite the fact that such guidance may ultimately be the most important factor in developing a value system. As discussed earlier, one's commitment to living a moral life depends, to a large degree, upon belief in the Almighty and that we, His creatures, matter to Him.

The Rebbe asked all educators – parents and teachers alike – to recognize that teaching children about their spiritual makeup and inherent responsibilities is the underpinning of all effective education. This is true especially in modern times when the very idea that we need to help children develop a "spiritual value system" seems like a quaint remnant of yesteryear.

We must teach children that they are endowed with a *neshamah*, a soul that is a direct spiritual link to the Almighty. We must teach that they are part of the Chosen

People, and that this is not just a distinction, but also a responsibility. We must teach them to take pride in their Jewish identity and in being actively involved with their heritage. All this is an integral part and the product of a strong spiritual value system.

The same can be said about educators' responsibility to guide a child's experience of religious ritual and custom so that it will have a joyous and long-lasting impact. Children should always associate religious activity with enjoyment, even if it is childish pleasure, and thus cherish those experiences and the memories they evoke.

Striving Toward Holiness

G-d tells us to sanctify our daily life (Leviticus 19:2), and to make the mundane – eating, drinking and working – holy. This *can* be done, because wherever we are, G-d is with us.

Immediately after G-d says we should sanctify our lives, the Torah continues, "You should fear your mother and father" (Leviticus 19:3). This implies that it is the parents – the child's first educators – who need to instill in their children that they are unique and need to sanctify the mundane in their daily life.

How do we educate toward a goal of sacredness? This comes through Shabbat, which the above verse continues with. Resting on this day, as G-d wanted of us, teaches us that He is the Creator and gives the world continued existence.[185]

The Yearning

Through a spiritually oriented approach to education, and using words that emanate from the heart, it is possible for a child to develop a deep desire to connect to G-d. Education can inspire a child to become passionate about Judaism, and that deep yearning to connect to G-d can become an integral part of their life.[186]

The Soul

It is crucial to discuss with children that they have a spiritual makeup, and a soul that is "a part of G-d"[187] that was present at Mount Sinai. For the soul, fulfilling Torah and its mitzvahs is its lifeline. With this insight, children will surely request that their central sustenance be given to them.[188]

Bearer of the Sacred

Even in the best of times, Jews have always been a minority that differed in countless aspects of daily life. Being able to hold their own in the face of overwhelming odds needs special reinforcement from childhood and onward. This is especially true in countries where there is freedom of religion, and where there are no external barriers separating the Jew from gentile. This leaves the road to assimilation wide open; often there is no sudden break with tradition, but rather a gradual deviation, step after small step.

To illustrate this idea, there is a well-known parable of a child who strayed from the road and soon found himself in the midst of the woods. He got there by making a small wrong step off the road, which led to another and yet another.

The conditions and environment in the United States, for example, call for even greater spiritual reinforcement for the Jewish child. This reinforcement needs to be of such strength and duration that the child will always be conscious of the fact that they are the bearer of the sacred tradition of Torah and mitzvahs, and that they belong to a people that is holy and different. For this to unfold, it is essential that from early childhood to adolescence, the child should receive a comprehensive and encompassing Jewish education.[189]

Strive to Grow

Educators need to instill in their students the idea that a growing young person must mature, aim high, and not be stationary in their accomplishments.

The children cannot be told, "Now that you have reached perfection for today, stop learning; in fact, you need not come to school tomorrow." On the contrary, even though they remember everything they were taught the day before, a living person needs to continuously grow and increase their knowledge, improve their character, behavior, and so forth.[190]

According to Their Level

After children conclude their studies and want to play ball, it would be inappropriate to tell them that it is frivolous behavior, or discourage them from play in any capacity. Indeed, because children naturally want to play ball, they should be taught that the activity of playing ball should be "for the sake of heaven."

Later, as children mature, they should be taught that in order to study Torah better, it is necessary to engage in physical exercise. Indeed, that may prove to be the most relevant and spiritually fulfilling message for their present spiritual standing.

As they grow older, they should be taught Torah sources that explain why it is permissible to play ball and the spiritual lessons one could learn from a ball, and so forth.[191]

185. *Likkutei Sichot*, vol. 1, p. 255.

186. Ibid, vol. 15, pp. 133 and 135.

187. *Tanya* ch. 2, beg.

188. *Torat Menachem 5748*, vol. 3, p. 472.

189. Letter from February 5, 1962.

190. *Torat Menachem 5744*, vol. 1, pp. 105-106.

191. *Sichot Kodesh 5740*, vol. 2, p. 819.

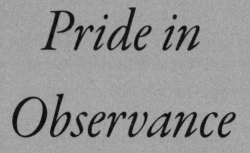

Pride in

Observance

t is one thing to be proud of one's heritage, and it is quite another to proudly commit to living in accordance with one's heritage. Instilling pride in living a devoutly Jewish life is one of the ultimate goals of Jewish education. And yet we live in a free world enjoying all its inherent liberties, so the question remains: How acculturated should we become? Should children raised in a typical Western milieu adopt all its cultural nuances, or is there an inherent distinction between how our children are raised and the prevailing culture?

Maintaining an atmosphere of Torah and mitzvahs is the objective of education and should be the primary goal of Jewish schools. Therefore, it follows that teaching children to feel proud of their Torah values must be the foundation of *all* curricula at school.

We should teach children that living a Jewish life is about the pursuit of its spiritual dimension – namely, seeking a spiritually meaningful path rather than indulging in the gratification of self-serving desires. This ought to be the goal of all educators, and it is achievable by helping children cultivate and be proud of their relationship with the Almighty.

The Rebbe was especially emphatic about the responsibility of both parents and teachers to ensure that the underlying message of all their educational endeavors instill a strong sense of pride and uncompromising dedication to Torah tradition.

The Importance

As a minority religion, it is natural to develop an inferiority complex in relation to the majority. Therefore, it is essential to ingrain in children, from the earliest age, a sense of pride in our heritage and customs, as well as a strong Jewish identity, so that instead of hiding their Jewishness, they can be proud of it without inhibitions. To develop this sense of pride, we must instill warm, positive feelings toward true Jewish values, inculcating in them a sense of deference to the spiritual realm.[192]

Being Yourself

A person cannot change the essence of who they are. For example, one can regularly choose to change their clothing, but they cannot change their nose on a whim. With this, a person should not shy away from who they are, and ought to act in accordance with their essence.

For a Jew, it should be obvious that they are proud to be Jewish. But there are those who argue: how can we influence the rest of the world if we show, like Haman in the Purim story argued, that our religion is different?

We learn the answer from the Book of Esther. Mordechai refused to bow to Haman. His purpose was not to anger the minister; rather, Mordechai simply wanted to act like a Jew, as per the essential tenets of G-d's commandments.

When Jews act in this way, threatening challenges are merely temporary, and in the end – as the biblical narrative continues – it brought honor to Mordechai. In fact, the monarch commanded the citizens of the land to assist the Jewish nation.

The lesson for parents is that that even if they live amongst non-Jews, teaching their child to shun their Jewishness, so as not to anger a neighbor, causes the child to act the opposite of their very nature.

However, when we care for children, we need to teach them to not hide who they are. Thus, when a child receives a candy, they first check to see if it is kosher, then say to their friend that they need to make a blessing. The child will explain that G-d created the world, and that the blessing is thanking the Creator, just like one would thank someone for giving them the candy. This will bring respect to the child for their refined behavior.[193]

192. *Moreh LeDor Nevoch*, p. 177.   193. *Torat Menachem 5742*, vol. 2, p. 954.

Spiritual

Development

n contrast to many educators who are concerned that using spiritual ideas when talking to children is futile at best, and perhaps counterproductive, the Rebbe felt that the innocence of children, and their ready acceptance of all matters, enables them to integrate deep ideas.

He taught that discussing the soul with children can be very impactful. In this capacity, an educator is able to impress upon children the concept of their own spirituality and connection to the Almighty.

On occasion, when he addressed children, the Rebbe appeared to discuss spiritual ideas that adults struggle to understand. He wanted Torah educators to follow suit.

Additionally, the Rebbe encouraged upperclassmen to engender responsibility toward their younger schoolmates. He instructed school officials to find ways to motivate older children to help teach younger students. The Rebbe would say metaphorically, "If you know *alef*, teach *alef*." He saw this as being advantageous to both the older and younger students, and a responsibility demanded of us all.

Permeating Daily Life

The educator's objective is to reveal the Divine soul within their students, so that it will permeate their entire essence. In daily life, there needs to be a common, immutable point that is in consonance with their Divine soul. In other words, everything the student sees and experiences was created, guided and is under the continued providence of G-d.

Regardless of their young age, this needs to be revealed to them, not as something new, but as something they already possess that is simply in a state of concealment. A good educator will find the right words to impress these matters upon children.

While their intellect is not well-developed, they still possess a complete Divine soul. Therefore, their conduct should be permeated with G-dliness, Torah and mitzvahs.[194]

Unending Flame

The indicator of a good education is that the flame kindled by an educator is able to thrive on its own. This means the student should not be dependent forever upon the encouragement of the educator, or continuously seek their answers every step along the way.[195]

Future Leaders

It is conceivable that students of higher grades can be trained as counselors, mentors and instructors for younger grades. To be sure, this is not a formal position, but rather an opportunity to accustom them to the idea of leadership and education.[196]

While at first they may not be successful, doing this even for a few hours will over time increase their motivation to be diligent and responsible, and fill their knowledge gap and pedagogic skills. Of course, this is not suitable for every student, but the opportunity should be considered for every student.[197]

194. *Torat Menachem 5745*, vol. 4, p. 2301.

195. *Torat Menachem 5746*, vol. 3, p. 519.

196. *Igrot Kodesh*, vol. 11, p. 206.

197. Ibid, vol. 15, p. 371.

Developing

Torah Passion

Torah study is the seminal obligation of every Jew; it transcends other religious requirements and is essential to leading a committed Jewish life.

The Torah introduces this commandment with an unusual statement. Rather than using a normative, direct statement, the Torah states, "And you shall teach them [the commandments] diligently *to your children*."[198] For in addition to one's personal obligation to study Torah, we must ensure that it is passed on to the next generation.

Throughout the millennia, teaching children was a fundamental preoccupation of all Jewish communities. The lives of children and adults revolved around the study of Torah. The popular description of Jews as "People of the Book" conveys not just our dedication to an intellectual pursuit, but reveals that "the Book" has made us who we are.

Parents are obligated to begin teaching their children to recite verses of Torah as soon as they are able to speak. The fact that children don't understand the words is irrelevant. What matters is the idea that is impressed upon them – that the study of Torah is of major importance in their lives.

This is not done by sitting our children down and

telling them that Torah is important, but rather by creating experiences for them that demonstrate its importance.

Teaching Affection

Even a young child who has not yet begun to study Torah should be taught to perceive its importance. To teach this, the child is brought to synagogue to kiss the Torah scroll lovingly, with the same affection that they embrace what is most precious to them, namely their parents.[199]

Prior to Understanding

Even prior to a child's formal education, a parent or sibling teaches them Torah verses in Hebrew or another language they understand best. When they subsequently learn and understand the words of Torah properly, they will be able to understand how it is connected to their daily life.[200]

Their Level

Young children need to have words of Torah explained to them in simple words so that they can understand. Nonetheless, this is not a license to misconstrue the Torah with fantastical or false tales.[201]

The Preoccupation

Parents should strive for their children – boys and girls – to quote words of Torah to the point that it becomes integrated into their identities.[202]

Gatherings

It is worthwhile to strengthen the custom of reciting a Torah thought when children gather together. This will further ingrain its teachings in their lives.[203]

Books as Gifts

It is highly appropriate to give Torah books as gifts – even to small children – on joyous occasions or before a holiday.[204]

198. Deuteronomy 6:7.

199. *Torat Menachem 5749*, vol. 1, p. 203.

200. *Torat Menachem 5751*, vol. 1, p. 156.

201. *Sichot Kodesh 5736*, vol. 2, p. 146.

202. *Sichot Kodesh 5728*, vol. 2, p. 430. See *Hilchot Talmud Torah*, end of chapter 1.

203. *Torat Menachem 5751*, vol. 1, p. 156.

204. *Torat Menachem 5752*, vol. 2, p. 76.

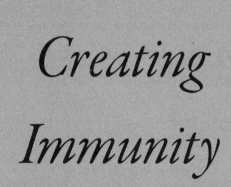

Creating

Immunity

M uch of the preceding material is based upon the premise that the environment in which children are raised has a powerful influence on them. By the time children reach their teens, peers and popular culture have greater influence than parents and the home environment. Families that expect to inculcate values, ethics and morals in their children have to consider carefully how to deal with the effects of their cultural setting since they may find themselves at odds with it.

When children are encouraged to make up their own minds about religious and moral issues – as opposed to the values of the community in which they were raised – traditional Jewish education is threatened gravely. The primary goal of Jewish education is to teach Torah values, ethics and morals that derive from the Word of G-d, and a way of life inspired by the Torah. Wider culture, however, does not encourage or facilitate – and sometime even opposes – these goals.

How should parents counter the cultural influences to which their children are exposed?

The Rebbe's position is that Jewish education is not the place for compromise between Torah values and prevailing culture. On the contrary, Jewish education must present a complete and undiluted view of Judaism.

The Rebbe explains that children must receive a clear message that their connection with the Almighty is an eternal, spiritual bond; thus, their education and initiation into Torah should not be limited by outside considerations.

Future Challenges

A common mistake that parents make is maintaining the hope that their children will independently reach a certain religious standard when they grow up. Therefore, they limit their children's education during childhood and adolescence. However, these parents fail to take into account that if they want their child to reach a certain standard when they become independent, then from an early age they need to develop tools to withstand the challenges that arise from their exposure to negative influences. With tools, children will be able to attain a healthy balance.

Another essential point one needs to take into account is the strong pressure and influence children are exposed to on a regular basis in school and in the community. When these influences are negative, parents need to provide their children adequate inoculation so that they can withstand these temptations.[205]

Feeling Cheated

When educators compromise, students see immediately that they are not being taught an inherent truth; rather, they are being treated in accordance with the winds of the time. However, when leniencies are discouraged, the students feel they are being given something fundamental and authentic, and not subject to whim. This in itself attracts people.[206]

The Seed

The Torah compares a person to a tree.[207] If a tree is scratched after it is already grown, the scratch only affects a limited area and doesn't harm the tree. But when a seed yet to be planted is injured, the tree that subsequently grows may well be severely damaged.

This is also true of education. If an adult who has already weathered a portion of their life feels the need to temporary compromise their Jewish practice, the impact will likely be time-limited. Previous years, and future years, will serve as a source of strength to enable them to move past the temporary fallout and return to complete Jewish observance.

However, when talking about children – and there are those who want to educate by making compromises from the get-go – it is important to understand that this approach may impact their passion and zeal for Judaism for their entire lifetime. An upbringing deficient in faith could, G-d forbid, affect them for life.[208]

Every Step

A person does not stray from a path and end up in the depths of a forest all at once; they start with one small step in the wrong direction. The sooner they catch themselves straying, the easier it will be to return to the correct path.

Therefore, it is important to return a child to the right path even at a young age, without compromise, for in the future, matters may be more difficult to correct. The same applies in the positive sense; each act of growth and improvement during childhood, even of the smallest kind, will lead to further development.[209]

The Passion

We should not forget that during teen years, for the most part, many children decrease in their Jewish observance relative to their parents. Thus, if parents provide their children a compromised Jewish education, where there is not enough warmth and passion, it will be compromised further in the next generation.

This is especially true in light of the challenges and difficulties experienced by younger generations. Therefore, they need to be given more tools that will strengthen their connection to Torah and mitzvahs.[210]

The Details

Our sages invested tremendous effort to ensure the purity of children's education. They waged war so that no detail would be compromised, even factors that seemed unimportant. They keenly understood that formative years impact a child's entire life, and that children must be armed with inner resilience to prevail over challenges they will encounter along their journey.[211]

205. *Likkutei Sichot,* vol. 38, p. 170. See *Moreh LeDor Nevoch*, p. 177.

206. *Torat Menachem,* vol. 14, pp. 136-137.

207. Deuteronomy 20:19. Cf. *Taanis* 7a.

208. *Torat Menachem*, vol. 10, p. 289.

209. *Likkutei Sichot*, vol. 20, pp. 645-646.

210. *Igrot Kodesh,* vol. 8, p. 18.

211. *Torat Menachem*, vol. 10, pp. 288-289.

The G-dly
Relationship

P raying to the Almighty is an integral part of Jewish life. One does not wait for a crisis in order to pray. Rather, one can pray in order to acknowledge G-d's presence, to thank Him for life and its blessings and, of course, when seeking Divine intervention. Children should be taught to pray as soon as they can speak full sentences.

Teaching children to pray is critical, as this is the first step in their personal connection with G-d. They need to learn that they can reach out to the Almighty – whom they can't see, hear or fully comprehend – and are able to communicate with Him through prayer. With proper education, they learn there is something sublime about prayer that allows them to touch a spiritual realm outside of their daily experiences.

Since the advent of the Chasidic movement, prayer has become a highly personalized, intellectual and emotional pursuit. Contemplating the nature of G-d, and His relationship to creation – human beings in particular – has helped make prayer a fervent and charged experience. In Chabad tradition, the Chasid should spend hours deep in thought before and during formal prayer.

Regardless of religious background, the Rebbe believed that all children should be taught to think about their relationship with G-d, in whatever manner. He maintained that a few moments of such contemplation are an antidote to the shiftless and aimless existence that plagues so many young people.

The Rebbe's interest was not limited to children growing up in Chasidic homes, nor only to children who were receiving a meaningful Jewish education. The Rebbe also discussed the plight of Jewish children in public schools who may lack basic Jewish education. These children are de facto deprived of their rightful connection to their heritage. He called on public schools to allow at least a moment of silence at the start of each day for children of all faiths to contemplate their relationship with G-d and to keep this "ember [of faith]" from being extinguished.

Routine of Thanks

While it is most important that a child study in a Jewish day school, at the very least, they should be encouraged to have a moment of daily prayer, so that the mentioning of G-d will be routine in the child's life.

Rabbi Israel Baal Shem Tov, founder of the Chasidic movement, would ask even young children about their wellbeing, so that that they would have an opportunity to thank G-d.[212]

Inspired to Contemplate

If a student is inspired to increase their focus in a positive area, even if its true meaning is beyond their grasp, they should be encouraged. Thus, the student who wants to place emphasis on their prayers should be allowed. However, they should be encouraged to focus properly so that their thoughts don't drift. This can be accomplished by supervising and offering guidance on what words, subjects and thoughts they should focus their attention.[213]

While their prayer may seem insincere, eventually this will increase their reverence for G-d and give them a tool to withstand the daily challenges outside of school, and remove them – even if only on a superficial level – from mundane desires. [214]

Home Recognition

A child should recognize in their daily life that food gives vitality to the body and becomes their flesh and blood, and that physical objects in their home – portrayed by the mezuzah on every doorpost – are from G-d, the source of all life.

To stress this, it is usual for children to kiss the mezuzah. By lifting the child to kiss it both during the day, especially upon awakening, and at the end of the day, before they go to sleep – it is apparent that the objects in the room, the room itself, and the entire home are connected to the One G-d. [215]

Thinking Prayer

Prayer is about thinking of G-d, and contemplating the meaning of the words. This is accomplished by looking into the prayer book, focusing on the intentions of the prayer, and reciting each word. [216]

212. *Igrot Kodesh,* vol. 22, p. 475.
213. *Igrot Kodesh,* vol. 14, p. 318.
214. Ibid, vol. 5, p. 325.

215. *Sefer HaSichot 5752,* vol. 1, p. 89.
216. *Torat Menachem 5743,* vol. 1, p. 144.

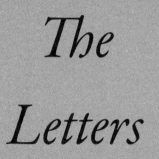

The

Letters

Since Talmudic times, our sages have taught us about mystical aspects contained in Hebrew letters. How they should be taught to children has always been a matter of concern for educators and religious leadership alike.

There have been proponents for pedagogically-inspired change, but the Rebbe cautioned, including to myself, against altering how the letters are taught and explained the reasoning behind a traditional approach.

Letters, Then Vowels

Our sages guide us to teach the letters separately from the vowels, and afterwards to combine them. Teaching this way ingrains in the child the essence of the *alef* that connotes *Alufo shel olam* – Ruler of the world – and the Hebrew word *Anochi*, the first word of the Ten Commandments, referring to G-d. But if the child begins to learn the letter *alef* with the vowel, the opportunity to implant these profound concepts in a child's heart has been missed.[217]

It is also acceptable to teach vowels to letters the child has already learned, before completing the entire Hebrew alphabet. However, it may be easier for a child to learn all the vowels together, after completing the alphabet. This is a question that classroom educators need to explore in regard to their students.[218]

Precise

The holiness of *alef bet* letters and vowels (*nekudot*) originate from Mount Sinai.[219] In kabbalistic sources, this applies to the names of the letters and vowels, which are acronyms of names of angels.[220]

The Vowels

The vowels should be taught per the order on the *alef bet* chart (as is printed in the prayer book). Aside from esoteric reasons, it is also recommended so as to not to confuse the children when they learn with different people, be it their parents or other educators.[221]

The Visuals

The printed letters should be true to their form, and not embellished, for this may impress the mind that embellished letters are the true form.[222]

Depending on what will be more effective in exciting the students' interest, the letters can be colorful or black-on-white.[223]

217. *Torat Menachem 5742*, vol. 4, p. 2123.
218. *Igrot Kodesh*, vol. 8, p. 39.
219. Note from the Rebbe: "As it states in several places in the *Zohar* and *Tikkunei Zohar*."
220. *Igrot Kodesh*, vol. 13, p. 93.
221. *Shaarei Halacha Ve'Minhag*, vol. 3, p. 197.
222. Ibid, p. 194.

223. *Igrot Kodesh*, vol. 23, p. 83. The Rebbe continues there: "One may want to use black letters so that they resemble the letters written in Torah scrolls and mezuzahs. However, it is noteworthy that the breastplate of the High Priest had individual letters engraved on colorful stones."

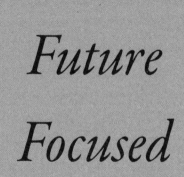

Future

Focused

The Rebbe stressed that mindful educational practice should not simply be focused on the moment but rather on the future – how a young person will be impacted over time. The objective of all instruction is to positively guide a young person for the long term. A superficial, reactive response will dissipate. Instead, we need to find a way to leave a lasting impression.

He also stressed that adults need to be forthright and honest with children, not only because children need to learn the value of honesty, but because if we are to have a moral influence on them, they need to know we are not equivocating. He taught us that if young people are to trust what we teach them, they must believe that we are conveying "truth" as we know it, not just what we want them to believe is truth.

So, in teaching central Jewish tenets, we should not impart only the concepts and practices that we think are fundamental, but also provide context for seemingly minor customs. The Rebbe reasoned that we may not fully appreciate how young people are profoundly impacted by spiritual matters.

We need to find the right words to convey the breadth of a religious concept without watering it down to the point that it loses meaning. The Rebbe often spoke of lofty ideas in simple words. He stressed that we must always speak to children in words that they can readily appreciate and use metaphors familiar to them. In other words, we must speak their language.

The Rebbe saw a human being as an amalgam of body and soul. Since body and soul are interdependent, for children to be healthy, they must be spiritually nourished as well. Torah is the key to their spiritual health; therefore, partial measures simply won't do.

The Maximum

We are told that a righteous woman named Kimchit merited seven sons who all served as high priests in the Holy Temple in Jerusalem. When asked why she merited this, she responded that she had been extra careful, beyond what is obligated, with modesty.[224]

Priesthood is passed down via paternal lineage, but Kimchit specifically wanted her children to be high priests. Why was this so important to her?

We learn that when one has the ability to maximize their child's potential – even to the high priesthood – this becomes their mission. And if one neglects the task, they have not fulfilled their G-d-given obligation.[225]

Health of the Spirit

Mothers who want their children to be physically, materially, and spiritually healthy, should understand that this depends upon the health of the soul. When there is serenity, the body can be healthy as well. For a Jew, a healthy spirit is dependent upon living according to Torah.

A mother may ask: What is the connection between a Torah life and physical health? A child's health is dependent on proper diet, sleep, and the like. What connection is there between the general health of a child and keeping kosher, saying blessings, praying and learning the *alef bet*?

It is important to understand that since the Almighty created the world, He is Master over both soul and body, and in the Torah He ruled that the two are interdependent.

For example, we know that a person who has engineered a factory knows better than anyone else how it should be run. There are details that may seem small and insignificant, but the engineer knows that each feature affects the entire factory. Similarly, a homemaker chooses to run their house in a specific manner, since they have insight into what is best for the household.

Thus, the general health of a child is improved when their spiritual education is complete and without compromise. This way, the child is raised with clear values that beget calmness, which leads to less anxiety and better overall health.[226]

The Custom

When young children become accustomed to Jewish customs from an early age, this often leaves a greater lifetime impact than formal instruction. This is especially true when the parent or teacher adds a story and explanation that brings depth to their understanding.[227]

The Angel's Candies

When the Rebbe Rashab, Rabbi Sholom Dovber, started school at the age of three, his grandfather showered him with candy and told him that the Angel Michael had thrown them, as per the popular custom.

To the young child, candies from an angel were precious indeed, and he saved them. Before Passover, when it is customary to check pockets for any leaven, his grandfather asked about the candies. Sholom Dovber had still not eaten them.

While leaven could be sold to a non-Jew, there is a custom to not sell something that was received from a rebbe. Thus, the Tzemach Tzedek told his young grandson to eat the candies.

We learn from this that every mitzvah, and even customs, should be performed authentically. Even when it is simple for a child to subdue their desires or perceived needs, they should be taught to follow the prevalent custom.[228]

224. The Talmud, *Yoma* 47a.

225. *Torat Menachem,* vol. 20, p. 69.

226. *Likkutei Sichot,* vol. 2, p. 574.

227. *Igrot Kodesh*, vol. 14, p. 71.

228. *Likkutei Sichot*, vol. 16, pp. 129, 138.

PART V

Twelve Essential Verses

Our sages taught millennia ago that what is committed to memory at an early age is not easily forgotten. The Rebbe introduced the idea of having children frequently recite, ponder, and memorize twelve Torah passages that express the core of Jewish belief and practice. Moreover, they represent the basic commitment and personal connection to G-d, which is the spiritual lifeline of every person.

Introducing the idea of reciting the passages in the spring of 1976, the Rebbe said that education is not only about wisdom and knowledge. It is also about teaching about daily life, even while eating, sleeping, and traveling.[229] Therefore, the good teacher's instruction is recognizable in their students at any time of day. The Rebbe said he would choose these verses, teaching the child to understand them well enough to be able to explain the ideas to a friend.

When instructed at their level, the Rebbe said, the child would recall the verses while playing and be able to conduct themselves appropriately.

Learning the verses would also encourage the child's natural enthusiasm in these areas. Because of this outward expression beyond their normal natural conduct, "it will not depart them," when they are older (Proverbs

22:6), and they will be able to go beyond their perceived limitations in their service to G-d.[230]

Presented here are the twelve verses explained by the Rebbe with introductions by my son, Rabbi Mendel Kaplan.

229. See Maimonides, *Mishneh Torah*, *Hilchot Deiot* 5:1.

230. *Sichot Kodesh 5736*, vol. 2, pp. 145 and 148ff.

תּוֹרָה צִוָּה לָנוּ
מֹשֶׁה מוֹרָשָׁה
קְהִלַּת יַעֲקֹב

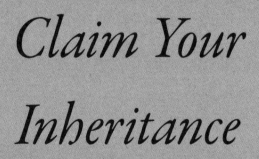

Claim Your

Inheritance

The Torah that
Moses commanded us
is the heritage of the
congregation of Jacob.

Deuteronomy 33:4

Judaism's spiritual treasure is your birthright. It is your inheritance; you just have to claim it.

The first question one may ask when staking a claim to Torah is, "How is Judaism relevant to me today?" This verse tells you that Judaism is not only relevant to you; it's *who you are*.

The Torah was given to every one of us through Moses, G-d's most faithful servant. Every Jew is entitled to inherit all of it. It's not exclusive to rabbis, scholars, or prophets. It naturally belongs to every single Jew. Each of our souls is like a letter in a Torah scroll, which is only complete when *all* the letters are included. But we need to all be present to achieve our potential as the Nation of Israel.

Everyone's Inheritance

The verse tells us that the Torah is our inheritance. Just as even a one-day-old child can acquire an inheritance, so too when a child is born, they inherit the Torah.

The inheritance, Torah, the verse tells us, belongs to the entire Jewish nation, "the house of Jacob." Jacob in Hebrew could mean the heel, meaning that even someone who is like the heel – the lowest common denominator – inherits the Torah.

G-d placed Himself in the Torah. Just like a person who inherits, so too we grasp the essence of G-d with the study of Torah.[231]

Even a Child

Our sages say that when a child begins to speak, they should be taught the above verse,[232] the starting point of their education.

Even a young child can understand that just as they value their toys and other prized possessions, so is the value of the Torah and what Torah is about.[233]

231. *Lekutei Sichot*, vol. 4, p. 1166 ff.
232. The Talmud, *Sukkah* 42a. *Mishneh*

Torah, Hilchot Talmud Torah 1:6.
233. *Sichot Kodesh 5736*, vol. 2, p. 146.

שְׁמַע יִשְׂרָאֵל
אֲ-דֹנָי אֱ-לֹהֵינוּ
אֲ-דֹנָי אֶחָד

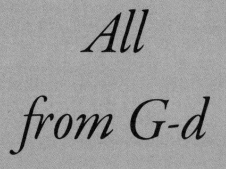

All

from G-d

Hear, O Israel,
the L-rd is our G-d,
the L-rd is One.

Deuteronomy 6:4

Do spiritual concepts and notions have anything to do with the real world? These ideas are actually what the real world is all about. Spiritual theory is concrete reality; G-d's presence is the truest reality and we must endeavor to sense the Divine in everyday life.

As we go about our physical existence, we may lose sight of the life force that makes it happen. The Jewish creed – the *shema* – is a reminder of that fact. The message that "G-d is One" means that the Divine presence is everywhere, ubiquitous throughout the magnificent creation.

All from One

The child should begin to learn the verses of the *shema* during the day and also at night from the earliest age possible, and should have them explained at their level of understanding.

This should include explaining that the Hebrew word for "one" has three letters: *alef*, *chet* and *daled*. The first letter *alef*, has the numerical value of one and is representative of the One G-d, our Creator, who has brought the universe into existence. The letter *chet*, the equivalent of eight, represents the seven upper worlds and earth, and the *daled*, the equivalent of four, represents the four cardinal points.

The adult should explain all this in a way appropriate to the child's understanding, and that, although they see the heavens, earth, and four directions as a part of nature, they should know that G-d – the "One" directs it all. Explaining this to a child will evoke a love of G-d.[234]

Revealing the One

The verse does not say that G-d is the single existence in our world. It tells us that the world is a true existence, where the Oneness of G-d can be felt. G-d is one with the world, a world that exists, and we need to reveal G-dliness in it.[235]

234. *Sichot Kodesh 5736*, vol. 2, pp. 146 and 148.

235. *Lekutei Sichot*, vol. 11, p. 11.

בְּכָל דּוֹר וָדוֹר חַיָּב
אָדָם לִרְאוֹת אֶת
עַצְמוֹ כְּאִלּוּ הוּא
יָצָא מִמִּצְרַיִם

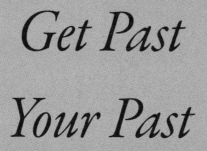

Get Past

Your Past

In every generation, one must view as if they personally went out of Egypt.

The Talmud, *Pesachim* 116b

Over 3,300 years ago, G-d delivered the Jewish people from Egypt. The Exodus was the transformation from slavery to freedom. Exodus still applies to us today; it is the freedom to be able to fulfill one's spiritual self. You just need to take the initiative to set yourself – your soul – free. Too many say that, having failed in the past, they carry the label of failure. But the past does not disable your present or future efforts.

Mitzrayim – the Hebrew word for Egypt, which literally means "narrow straits" – is not merely a place that we left in antiquity; it conveys the idea of deeper "inner limitations." Our struggle with internal self-doubt and fear prevents self-actualization and stunts our spiritual growth. It was one thing for us to get out of Egypt, but it's another to get the Egypt mentality out of us. It means breaking away from our past failings and transcending our circumstances instead of helplessly being held prisoner.

Still Slaves

The Torah tells us that the story of Exodus should be told to our children.[236] On Passover, we tell them that if it was not for G-d, we would still be in Egypt, that "we would still be slaves there now."[237] Being free evokes love for the Almighty, and the child will want to do what G-d wants.[238]

No Longer Slaves

We need to remember that we are no longer slaves in Egypt. When evil inclines us to act as the Egyptians acted, we banish the thoughts with the knowledge, "G-d took us out of Egypt. We are now a holy nation and have no connection to their ways."[239]

---

236. *Haggadah,* sec. beg. "*baruch haMakom.*"
237. The *Haggadah.*

238. *Sichot Kodesh 5736,* vol. 2, p. 147.
239. *Der Rebbe Redt Tzu Kinder,* vol. 1, p. 275.

כָּל יִשְׂרָאֵל יֵשׁ לָהֶם
חֵלֶק לְעוֹלָם הַבָּא,
שֶׁנֶּאֱמַר: וְעַמֵּךְ
כֻּלָּם צַדִּיקִים
לְעוֹלָם יִירְשׁוּ אָרֶץ,
נֵצֶר מַטָּעַי מַעֲשֵׂה
יָדַי לְהִתְפָּאֵר

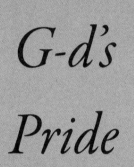

G-d's
Pride

All Israel has a share
in the world to come,
as it is stated: "And
Your people are all
righteous. They shall
inherit the land
forever. They are the
branch of My planting,
the work of My hands,
in which I take pride"
(Isaiah 60:21).

The Talmud, *Sanhedrin* 90a

You may feel distant from the key concepts of formal Judaism, finding it is too restrictive and full of old ideas. How can you possibly relate to it? But it is not alien to you. You have inherited a slice of eternity, waiting to be nurtured. Eternity is already in your hands. You just need to keep improving your natural spiritual strengths.

Our sages taught that G-d takes immense pride in and cares deeply about every member of the Nation of Israel, like a gentle gardener tending all of their plants. Each of us is born with an intrinsic gift of eternal reward. When we appreciate our precious gift of life, pursue a higher purpose and meaningfully develop our spiritual potential, we gain a portion of eternity.

A Part of Eternity

Our sages emphasize that everyone, including our children, should know that we are "the work of My hands, in which I take pride." Even a child understands that as much as their parents are physically bigger, G-d is incomparably great. Despite this, they are "the work" of G-d's "hands." And because of this they will inherit a part of the eternal world where there are no limits of time.

By thus connecting to G-d, they themselves become limitless. It should be explained to them that it is up to them to choose who to be with, those who veered from the correct path or with the great sages."[240]

You Never Know

A person might ask why they need to dedicate themselves to others when they could use their time for personal study. Our sages emphasize that everyone has a portion of the next world. This does not differentiate between people, and one may never know who is truly on a greater spiritual level. Only in the next world is it possible to see which person is greater than another.[241]

240. *Sichot Kodesh 5736*, vol. 2, p. 147.   241. *Lekutei Sichot*, vol. 1, p. 262.

כִּי קָרוֹב אֵלֶיךָ

הַדָּבָר מְאֹד בְּפִיךָ

וּבִלְבָבְךָ

לַעֲשׂתוֹ

It's

Easy

It is exceedingly close
to you, in your mouth
and heart, to do it.

Deuteronomy 30:14

The pessimist looks at the task ahead and says it's too difficult. The optimist believes that they can do it. To be able to achieve, we need to have a positive and optimistic outlook.

The idea of living a life dedicated to Torah can at times seem daunting. How can one maintain the discipline that the Torah demands? This verse teaches that the word "impossible" needs to be changed to "I'm possible."

The Rebbe wanted to inculcate into the mind of a child – and an adult, for that matter – to *never* think that full adherence to the Torah way of life is impossible to achieve. By definition, we accept that a personal G-d never demands anything of us without giving us the strength to achieve it. If every one of us is expected to live a Torah life, then it simply can't be impossible. Thus, it must be within our reach – "exceedingly close to you" – to fulfill the Torah's expectations.

This verse teaches us that we have a great spiritual reservoir, and even if it seems a bit overwhelming, the treasure of Judaism is closer to us than we think.

Feeling Close

The Torah tells us that Judaism is exceedingly close and easy to observe. What's more, it is close to one's heart. This needs to be explained to a child. Though they are drawn to their toys and to play, they need to know that Torah is close to them, too. If they would only contemplate the value of Judaism, they will see this for themselves.[242]

---

242. *Sichot Kodesh 5736*, vol. 2, p. 147.

וְהִנֵּה הַשֵּׁם נִצָּב
עָלָיו וּמָלֵא כָּל
הָאָרֶץ כְּבוֹדוֹ
וּמַבִּיט עָלָיו וּבוֹחֵן
כְּלָיוֹת וָלֵב, אִם
עוֹבְדוֹ כָּרָאוּי

Always

There

Behold G-d stands
over them – and the
whole earth is full
of His glory – and
searches their minds
and hearts [to see] if
they are serving Him
as is fitting.

R. Schneur Zalman of Liadi,
Tanya, Ch. 41

s personal observance necessary? People feel they are busy, that their time for Judaism is limited. The truth is that each of us has a unique contribution to make, and in the eyes of the Almighty, there is nobody quite like you.

Rejecting the notion of a powerful but distant Creator, we believe in a close and *personal* G-d. He is never too busy running the universe. He has time to be deeply concerned about every individual who is navigating daily challenges.

The verse tells us that G-d searches our minds and hearts to see if we are doing what is right. In every place, at every moment, we must sense that G-d is standing close by, examining our thoughts, speech, and actions, empowering us to make the right choices in life. These thoughts should fill us with feelings of deep reverence and responsibility.

G-d's Reliance

The passage tells us that whatever state a person may be in, G-d "stands over them." The Hebrew could be translated as "that they take the place."[243] This means that G-d is concerned about the person's conduct, and what is happening internally to them.

"They are serving Him as is fitting" for G-d to have a place to dwell in this world. Even for a small child, this idea can have a huge impact.[244]

Joy in Closeness

In every army, the general is in one place and the soldiers in another. Yet, But/Yet? G-d is with us all the time, giving us all attention, knowing all that is happening to us. There are no police watching, but there is an Ear that hears and an Eye that sees, for G-d is always with us. This gives us the power to do what is right. This is done happily, for the great Creator choses always to be with us. When there is happiness, possibilities are limitless.[245]

243. See Kings I 22:40, where the word *nitzvav*, means that they *took the place* of the king.

244. *Sichot Kodesh 5736*, vol. 2, p. 148.
245. *Der Rebbe Redt Tzu Kinder*, vol. 1, p. 286.

בְּרֵאשִׁית בָּרָא
אֱ-לֹהִים אֵת
הַשָּׁמַיִם וְאֵת הָאָרֶץ

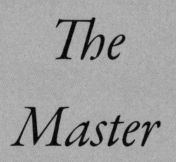

The

Master

In the beginning, G-d created the heavens and the earth.

Genesis 1:1

The world seems a dysfunctional mess. War, poverty, crime, terrorism and hatred are rampant. Can we ever know peace?

The Torah opens with a Divine act; all creation has a sacred purpose. The world was created broken but we can repair and perfect it. We have the capacity to be partners in making it a place of spiritual peace and perfection – a dwelling place for the Divine – releasing the world's potential for goodness.

Knowing this magnificent plan can lift our spirits even when we feel overwhelmed. It can make us realize that the world is predisposed to goodness for us all. But the specific task of discovering and accomplishing the world's holy potential is *our* duty and responsibility.

Overcoming Shock

Filled with chaos and negativity, our sages refer to the wold as "desolate."[246] One can be shocked by all around them. Thus, the verse tells us that us that the heavens and all that are in them, and the land and all that is on it, were created by G-d. There is a Master of the world who gave us the Torah so that we can lead the world and bring blessing and success.[247]

Daily Recognition

When the child recognizes that G-d created the world, the daily blessings at mealtime become a mission of revealing light, seeing G-dliness in the everyday. In this way they bring more light into their surroundings.[248]

Refraining Tool

When the child has knowledge of the Creator, it is easier to follow G-d's wishes. If evil urges them to forgo a blessing over their food, they can easily tell themselves that it is the voice of a fool. "Don't you know that G-d created this food," they will now think, "and I need to thank Him for it." The same is true when a friend tells them to do something wrong; they now have the means to answer them.[249]

Activities United

Both Torah study and prayers, "heaven," and our activities on "earth" are created by G-d. Thus, the mundane should be imbued with the spiritual light from our study and prayer.[250]

246. The Talmud, *Yevamot* 62b.

247. *Der Rebbe Redt Tzu Kinder*, vol. 1, p. 262.

248. Ibid, p. 23.

249. Ibid, p. 291.

250. Ibid, p. 295.

וְשִׁנַּנְתָּם לְבָנֶיךָ

וְדִבַּרְתָּ בָּם בְּשִׁבְתְּךָ

בְּבֵיתֶךָ וּבְלֶכְתְּךָ

בַדֶּרֶךְ וּבְשָׁכְבְּךָ

וּבְקוּמֶךָ

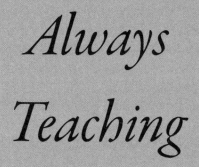

Always

Teaching

And you shall teach your children, and speak about it at home and during travel, when you go to sleep and wake up.

Deuteronomy 6:7

We are all teachers for the Almighty. Students are our children.[251] Every moment can be a chance to positively influence others. This is how we can help repair the world: one day at a time, one person at a time, one relationship at a time.

Communicating Torah teachings and ideals – sometimes directly and sometimes vicariously – is how we can uplift those around us. If we strive to punctuate our social interactions with encouraging, Torah-based conversation, then every moment can become a teachable moment.

It seems preposterous that a single person among billions can change the world. When you accept responsibility to educate those within your sphere of influence, though, to be a beacon of light, as our sages say, even one candle of truth can dispel much darkness and be seen from afar.[252] That's how we ultimately transform ourselves, our family and friends, and the wider world.

Constant Study

When educating a child, or anyone, what you want to teach should be an integral part of their daily life – their heart and mind. In this way, it will always be reviewed by them, even after school, at home, on travels, when they go to sleep and when they wake up. This will also lead them to want and ask their parents to study with them,[253] and to always have with them a Torah book or booklet to study.[254]

Young Educator

The student, our sages say, is like a child. The young child should be instructed in a way that they understand and are able to teach to others. In addition, this positive act will also have a greater impact on their thinking, speech, and action.[255]

251. *Sifri* and *Rashi* on the verse.

252. *Chovat Halevavot, Shaar Yichud Hamaaseh* ch. 5 and *Tanya* ch. 12.

253. *Der Rebbe Redt Tzu Kinder*, vol. 1, p. 262.

254. Ibid, p. 297.

255. Ibid, p. 298.

יָגַעְתִּי וְלֹא מָצָאתִי
– אַל תַּאֲמִין,   לֹא
יָגַעְתִּי וּמָצָאתִי –
אַל תַּאֲמִין, יָגַעְתִּי
וּמָצָאתִי תַּאֲמִין –

Keep

Climbing

"I have worked hard and not been successful." Don't believe them. "I have not worked hard but have been successful." Don't believe them. "I have worked hard and have been successful." Believe them.

The Talmud, *Megillah* 6b

Too many well-intentioned people expect things to go smoothly. They know their heart is in the right place and that they are doing the right thing, but they become quickly frustrated if things don't go as planned. There is an old saying: "When the going gets tough, the tough get going."

Our sages tell us that you know what to do, and you have the capacity to do it. Therefore, don't be distracted by a bump in the road or by the perceived lack of success. Continue to push forward and ultimately you will succeed.

Think of the "butterfly effect," whereby the flapping of a single butterfly's wings can theoretically change the weather. Our actions, however small, can become the tipping point for enormous positive change. Our combined efforts will always be successful and will prevail, even if we can't imagine how.

Uninformed Feelings

The child, thinking they should confess to some wrongdoing, may grow despondent, asking themselves, "How can I have fallen so low?"

They will then recall what our sages say that had they put in adequate effort, they would have succeeded in doing what was right. It will then dawn upon them that their misbehavior is just a minor lapse and not some deep flaw, and they will not feel discouraged.[256]

Constant Growth

A person should constantly be on the lookout for how to grow, to be better, to do another mitzvah. If one makes the effort, they will surely be successful. When seeing success, overcoming obstacles will be easier. This will remind you that it is not a time to do less, but to do more.[257]

Torah Belief

The above adage can be translated as that "the Torah believes that every person will make the effort and thus be successful." Every person has the potential to know what to do and how to act, and ultimately to do the right thing. Thus, when they decide to act, they will come through.[258]

256. *Der Rebbe Redt Tzu Kinder*, vol. 1, p. 263.

257. Ibid, p. 300.

258. Ibid, p. 301.

וְאָהַבְתָּ לְרֵעֲךָ כָּמוֹךָ
– רַבִּי עֲקִיבָא
אוֹמֵר, זֶה כְּלָל
גָּדוֹל בַּתּוֹרָה

Service
for Others

On the verse, "Love your fellow as yourself" (Leviticus 19:18), Rabbi Akiva said, "this is a great basic principle of the Torah."

Jerusalem Talmud, *Nedarim* 9:4

Some mitzvahs are between us and G-d, while others are between one person and another. Both are critical; neither can be neglected. If we don't love others, then we don't properly love G-d, for G-d loves them. If our own spiritual fulfillment is a desirable goal, then we also need to encourage and support the same goal in others.

Even at a young age, the child needs to recognize that it's not enough to only think about oneself. We need to think of others just as much as we think of ourselves. Simply put, if we want to succeed, we must help others be successful.

While a child may not be able to share material assistance in a significant way, they could share their wisdom, understanding, and knowledge with others, as well as our passion for Jewish life.

The Same Effort

The child should internalize the idea that just as one needs to make the effort for themselves, they need to make the effort for others.[259]

Action

To love your neighbor is not just a feeling of the heart nor an expression of words; it needs to be realized in action. Just as you would for yourself, you should extend yourself to help another, be it with money or in some other way.[260]

Feeling Sameness

At times we might feel that if we performed some kindness, we might now feel better than the other. But love is not only about doing good but also about refraining from slighting. Being kind does not mean that we can disrespect another.

In addition, even if you very much want what another person has, it does not become yyours. Being kind means that we should not try to outbid another in purchasing an item the other wants. This is what our sages say, that what you don't like being done to you, you must not do unto another.[261] If you would not tolerate it being done to you, don't do it to another.[262]

259. *Der Rebbe Redt Tzu Kinder*, vol. 1, p. 264.

260. Ibid, p. 304.

261. The Talmud, *Shabbat* 31a.

262. *Der Rebbe Redt Tzu Kinder*, vol. 1, p. 306.

וְזֶה כָּל הָאָדָם
וְתַכְלִית בְּרִיאָתוֹ
וּבְרִיאַת כָּל
הָעוֹלָמוֹת, עֶלְיוֹנִים
וְתַחְתּוֹנִים, לִהְיוֹת
לוֹ יִתְבָּרֵךְ דִּירָה זוֹ
בְּתַחְתּוֹנִים

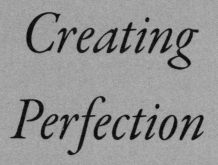

Creating

Perfection

The purpose of the creation of every person and of all the worlds – upper and lower – is to make a dwelling place for G-d in this lowest world.

Tanya, Ch. 33

Rather than viewing the world as an immense obstacle course, we need to comprehend that G-d created this world imperfectly so that we could perfect it. By living a righteous life and by striving to inspire others, we can transform the world into the sacred dwelling place it was meant to be.

Like Your Home

Just as you enjoy the comforts of your own home, you were created to make a home for G-d in our world. G-d's furniture is the mitzvahs He gave us.[263]

The Proper Home

A true home is when all those who go there know whose home it is. Thus, it is our mission to bring to others Jewish observance and to be a living example of a G-dly life.[264]

263. *Der Rebbe Redt Tzu Kinder*, vol. 1, p. 264.

264. Ibid, p. 22.

יִשְׂמַח יִשְׂרָאֵל
בְּעוֹשָׂיו, פֵּרוּשׁ
שֶׁכָּל מִי שֶׁהוּא
מִזֶּרַע יִשְׂרָאֵל יֵשׁ
לוֹ לִשְׂמֹחַ בְּשִׂמְחַת
הַשֵּׁם, אֲשֶׁר שָׂשׂ
וְשָׂמֵחַ בְּדִירָתוֹ
בַּתַּחְתּוֹנִים

Feel

the Joy

What the verse states, "Israel will rejoice in its Maker" (Psalms 149:2), means that every Jew should share in G-d's joy, Who rejoices and is delighted in His dwelling place in this world.

Tanya, Ch. 33

When participating in G-d's master plan for creation, you won't realize your true potential if you do not find joy in it. The happier we are, the more successful we are likely to be in our G-d-given mission.

Jews make up but one-fifth of one percent of the world's population. When contemplating that the Creator chose *you* to be a part of this tiny group that participates in the greatest mission in history, it is an overriding source of joy.

The Creator's Delight

A mitzvah should not only be done with delight because G-d chose us to do His will, but also because the Almighty rejoices with us too.[265]

265. *Der Rebbe Redt Tzu Kinder*, vol. 1, p. 265.

PART VI

Stages
of Education

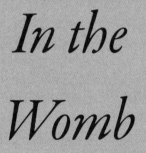

In the

Womb

n gestation, it is not only the body of the child that is forming, but also their spiritual dimension. Torah sources teach us that even behavior during intimacy impacts the yet-to-be conceived embryo. Therefore, the Rebbe frequently spoke about the need for parents to be acutely aware of influences on their offspring even throughout conception and pregnancy. Talmud, Jewish code, and Chasidic literature are replete with discussions of how parental behavior affects an unborn baby's spiritual and physiological makeup.

The observance of Family Purity brings a sense of sanctity into the marriage and by extension, to the unborn offspring. The Rebbe spoke strongly about this subject and charged his emissaries with the responsibility of educating others.

In a culture that often equates freedom with decadence and licentiousness, Family Purity provides an anchor, linking spiritual values to down-to-earth behavior in a relationship. The observance of these laws makes us acutely aware of our responsibility for our spiritual well-being as well as the health of future generations. Some parents choose to see this as limiting, while others see it as a privilege and solemn responsibility.

In the same vein, it has always been Jewish custom to

look for opportunities to make us worthy of G-d's blessing. We are taught that our actions and good deeds are directly connected to expression of His mercy. Childbirth is no different, and rabbinic literature has a great deal of such advice. The Rebbe cited a number of special mitzvahs that have a role in helping assure that the occasion-to-be is free of complications.

Education In Utero

Education begins before a child emerges into the world, during pregnancy and even before, for the preparations consist of being careful about the laws of purity and behavior during intimacy.

Chasidism teaches that an integral component of the child's makeup, namely what it refers to as the "garments" – the intrinsic nature of thought, speech, and deed – are determined by the measure of sanctity practiced by parents at the time of their child's conception.[266]

Food Health

The flesh and blood of the parents is created from their food and drink, and thus their consumption affects the child's character.[267]

Bringing Light

The light and holiness of the Shabbat has been cited as having a positive spiritual effect upon children, including candle lighting, which is entrusted to the mother.[268]

Additional Observances

Charity

An expectant mother, in addition to her regular contributions, should give a few extra coins to charity each weekday morning. Additionally, before candle lighting, she should contribute even a small amount, such as an additional 18 pennies, to a charity in Israel, in memory of the Tannaitic sage known as Rabbi Meir the Miracle-maker.[269]

Checking Mezuzahs

It is a good idea to check all the mezuzahs on the doorposts in the home and replace any that are not good with ones that are.[270]

Psalm 20

Without making an oath to do so, every night before reciting the Shema prayer, the father-to-be should recite Psalm 20. Once he has completed the entire recitation, he should repeat the opening two verses and have in mind, while he is reciting this, that G-d should consider it as if he had contemplated lofty thoughts that are appropriate at that time.[271]

266. *Torat Menachem 5744,* vol. 2, p. 1319. See *Tanya* ch. 2.

267. *Torat Menachem 5744,* vol. 2, p. 1319. See *Tanya,* ch. 8.

268. *Torat Menachem 5744,* vol. 2 p. 1319.

269. *Igrot Kodesh,* vol. 5, p. 327. Cf. ibid.

270. Ibid, vol. 6, p. 105.

271. Ibid, vol. 4, p. 454.

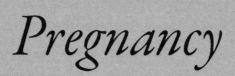

Pregnancy

The Rebbe encouraged privacy during the first stages of pregnancy. Staying out of the public eye while a fetus gestates is not just practical advice; it also has religious underpinnings. It is not merely a matter of "evil eye" and jealousy, for Jewish tradition holds that Divine blessings are more apt to be bestowed upon one who maintains privacy.

Rather, even though the baby is still in utero, the Rebbe counselled parents to be aware of their physical environment, since it has a spiritual impact on those living within it.[272] Therefore, imbuing the physical environment with spirituality by bringing words of Torah into it can only have a beneficial effect on the unborn fetus. Indeed, the Rebbe taught that the environment should be so pure that even a Torah scroll could be brought into it.

The same is true of the child's entry into the world. Introducing a spiritual dimension to childbirth can have only a positive impact on both mother and newborn.

The Oath

The sages say that the fetus does not leave the womb until it swears that it will "be righteous and not be wicked."[273]

Jewish law states that one cannot make an oath about something that does not exist. At that point, there is only a soul, and not yet an independent body capable of observing Torah, so the very concept of serving G-d and fulfilling mitzvahs has not yet come into existence.[274]

It is explained that the above dictum alludes to the fact that this oath is also elicited from the parents of each and every child, which obligates them to do everything in their power to help their child be righteous.

Of course, when the child will be an adult, they will have to rely on themselves to do what is right. However, the education that the child receives is up to the parents.[275]

Early Pregnancy

Until the mother enters the fifth month of pregnancy, it should not be publicized. This does not include informing people to whom one is very close.[276]

Psalm of Praise

The long-standing custom is to hang up small signs with Divine names and Scriptural verses, such as Psalm 121, the *Shir HaMaalot*, in the home of the woman giving birth. This has a spiritual effect on the birthing process, so that it be smooth and without complications. The practice also elicits blessings for a good and long life.[277]

Holy Atmosphere

Even what a day-old baby sees and hears is absorbed and has an impact as they grow older. In fact, scientific research has noted this as well, and includes the period of pregnancy.

Therefore, the chapter of Psalms mentioned above should be hung when the child is born and for the duration after, for as soon as a newborn breaths the air of this world, they will be surrounded with holiness. This brings blessing and success so that the parents will merit to raise the child to Torah, marriage, and good deeds.

With this message internalized, hanging the Psalms in the birthing room calms the mother and lifts her spirits. When this is explained to the doctor and hospital staff, they will agree to permit this custom.[278]

272. For example, Jewish law does not permit praying in an unsanitary or spiritually impure place.

273. The Talmud, *Niddah* 30b.

274. The Rebbe Rayatz, *Sefer Hasichot 5704*, p. 50.

275. *Torat Menachem*, vol. 29, p. 259.

276. *Likkutei Sichot*, vol. 12, p. 178.

277. *Torat Menachem 5747*, vol. 2, p. 38.

37. In regard to the importance of Jewish customs, see *Menachot* 20b, *Tosafot*, s.v. *nifsal. Maharil*, cited in *Rema* on *Yoreh Dei'ah,* 376:4.

278. *Torat Menachem 5747*, vol. 2, p. 38.

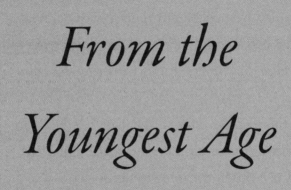

From the

Youngest Age

ublic relations specialists know that we are influenced by subliminal messages and impacted by things we see and hear without even taking notice thereof. Since everything leaves its mark, billions of dollars are spent on reaching audiences subconsciously.

Our sages teach that we are also impacted by our environment in spiritual ways that we cannot readily perceive. Creating an atmosphere of encouragement builds self-confidence in children. Similarly, when parents create an atmosphere of spiritual awareness, eschewing personal indulgence and instead practicing self-control, they endow their offspring with spiritual nourishment that the children will retain into adulthood.

The Rebbe also spoke about visual and tactile objects a child encounters. He suggested that an infant not come into contact with a non-kosher animal, and that their room be decorated exclusively with animals that are kosher as part of an environment that is in sync with Torah values.

Additionally, the Rebbe taught us that mitzvahs performed in the presence of children, or charitable contributions given on their behalf, impact them spiritually as well.

Furthermore, both Jewish law and Chasidic literature discuss the idea that what we consume has a spiritual effect upon our soul in the same way it affects the body. Just as the nutrients absorbed impact the body, the soul is similarly impacted by our food choices. Thus, adherence to strict standards of *kashrut* is as important for children as it is for adults.

The Atmosphere

The Torah tells us that as soon as a baby emerges into the world, they are influenced by everything happening around them. It is understood that an infant is influenced by the food and drink it consumes, for that nourishment become its flesh and blood. In addition, all that happens in the environment surrounding the baby influences the baby's soul. This includes the personal conduct of the parents.[279]

Thus, one should make an effort that the child be in a Jewish environment, one of Torah and mitzvahs, and surrounded with holy objects.[280]

The Effect

It is cited in Torah that whatever one sees and hears is engraved in an infant's brain and has a life-long effect. This is important during all stages of education.[281]

There is a common practice to hang images of non-kosher animals, such as dogs, cats, lions, and so on, in an infant's room.

Rather than seeing these images, our children should have a charity box, prayer book, Shema prayer, or the Hebrew alphabet.[282] This way, when the child looks around, they see things related to Torah. These items should be bright and colorful, in order to be pleasing to a child.

At first, the baby will merely glance at these holy objects, and later come the hand motions. When the child begins to talk, they will take an interest in these items. It will then be explained to them that we have the Torah, and that Torah is the greatest gift, and when the child grows up, they will more fully understand what it means.[283]

The Speech

Instilling a G-dly outlook begins the moment a baby is born, when the parents surround them with blessings, praise, and thanks to the Almighty for the child's movements, development, and the general delight the child evokes.[284]

279. *Torat Menachem 5742*, vol. 4, p. 2190.

280. *Torat Menachem 5743*, vol. 3, p. 1217.

281. *Torat Menachem 5744*, vol. 1, p. 487.

282. In a room where one gets undressed, prayer books and the like should be double-covered.

283. *Sichot Kodesh 5736*, vol. 2, p. 170.

284. *Torat Menachem 5741*, vol. 1, p. 316.

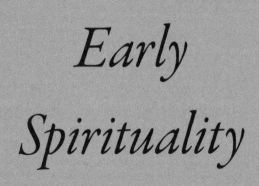

Early

Spirituality

One of the pillars of Judaism is belief in the *neshamah*, the Divine soul with which we are endowed and that bonds us with the Almighty. We are gifted with a soul at birth, and it is impacted by our behavior throughout life.

Regardless of our understanding of spirituality, it is real, and we can never divorce ourselves from our intrinsic spiritual dimension. The body and soul are inexorably bound together.

It is not only our corporeal being that impacts the *neshamah*, but also our behavior and environment. Therefore, it is our responsibility to ensure that our physical being and environment are synchronized with the spiritual needs of our soul. Adherence to Torah and its precepts helps us achieve this goal.

In the passages that follow, the Rebbe discusses how children, and even infants, are impacted by their environment, from the room they sleep in to the food they eat. It is incumbent upon us, says the Rebbe, to create a spiritually wholesome world for our children and thus positively impact their souls.

Stages of Entry

The beginning of our service of G-d begins from our first breath of air, when a holy soul enters the body. From that time, as the child grows, receives their formal education, and so forth,[285] the soul continues to have a greater role in the body, until the body itself becomes holy.[286]

Soothing Lullabies

It is proper to continue the age-old custom to soothe babies to sleep with songs and lullabies about the greatness of Torah, such as, "*Di Torah iz der beste sechoreh*," a soothing song speaking of Torah as the best "merchandise." This is done well before they know how to talk, or distinguish good from bad.[287]

Synagogue Sounds

The Talmud tells us that when Rabbi Yehoshua ben Chananya was still a baby, his mother would take him to synagogue to hear the sounds of Torah.[288]

From her, we learn that education begins when a baby is still in the cradle, even if it is just hearing words of Torah.[289]

Letter in a Torah Scroll

When a child is born, understandably the child cannot personally purchase a part in a Torah scroll. Thus, the parents should do it. Since what the baby hears and sees has an imprint on the future, the purchase should be done in front of the child.[290]

285. See, R. Schneur Zalman, *Code of Jewish Law (Later Edition)*, end of ch. 4.

286. *Torat Menachem 5751*, vol. 1, p. 315.

287 *Sichot Kodesh 5741*, vol. 1, p. 246.

288. Jerusalem Talmud, *Yevamot* 1:6.

289. *Likkutei Sichot*, vol. 23, p. 258.

290. *Ot Besefer Torah*, p. 50.

Beginning

of Formal

Education

As we have read, the Rebbe's recommendations regarding childrearing include the baby's earliest experiences, but when does formal education begin?

Early childhood educators know that formal education starts years before reading readiness. From a religious perspective, it begins when children are formally introduced to Jewish observance. When they are capable of understanding a mitzvah on a very basic level, they should be taught how to perform it, even if full understanding is years away.

With that in mind, we shall discuss the Rebbe's recommendations, sourced in Kabbalah and Chasidic philosophy, regarding what a child should actually be taught to do.

Reciting blessings is of the most common Jewish rituals. Saying a blessing creates awareness of our relationship with the Almighty, gives us pause to ponder the wonders of nature, and adds meaning to the performance of all mitzvahs. Having said that, what could be the possible benefit of teaching children to recite a blessing?

The most obvious reason for this is to prepare children from their earliest youth for religious observance in adulthood.

Teaching the Young

While considerable attention is given to educating older children, education of younger children is taken more lightly.

This attitude is rather surprising, for the Torah has clear views on the role of children in Jewish society. There is a clear ruling laid down by our sages that as soon as a child begins to speak, the parent should begin teaching them Torah.

True, there is great distance between a pre-verbal toddler and the Torah received at Sinai by Moses, who was 80-odd years old and at the height of his greatness.

Yet, this is precisely what the sages had in mind when they instructed that the verse, "Moses prescribed the Torah to us, an eternal heritage" (Deuteronomy 33:4), be of the first taught to children.

Just as in matters of inheritance where the age of the receiver is less consequential, we aim to connect the toddler to the Torah that was received at Sinai.[291]

Ingrained Kiss

Parents in a Jewish home should make sure that a child kisses the mezuzah on their bedroom doorpost before going to sleep. This conveys the idea that G-d is protecting them and everything in their room.[292]

Morning Appreciation

There is a custom to teach a child to recite *Modeh Ani*, thanking G-d for returning the soul in the morning, when they begin to talk – and some say it with the baby on their behalf from an even earlier age.[293]

Grace After Meals

The Grace After Meals should be taught in a manner that the child can understand, which will give them, from an early age, an appreciation that G-d is the source of their daily sustenance.[294]

The custom to recite at least 100 blessings daily[295] applies even to children, so that they will become accustomed to reciting the blessings to the point that it becomes second-nature.

This is also applicable to the *"amen"* response after someone else recites a blessing.

It is also important to remain conscious of G-d at all times through the blessings they recite; therefore, children should be taught the meaning of the blessings.[296]

291. Letter from July 30, 1973, *Letters to My Father*, p. 25. See Rabbi Schneur Zalman of Liadi, the laws of Torah study, ch. 1.

292. *Torat Menachem 5747*, vol. 2, pp. 647-648. As the *Zohar* states (*Zohar* 3:263b, 266b) the mezuzah protects people even when they leave their home.

293. *Torat Menachem 5742*, vol. 2, p. 708; and *Torat Menachem 5749*, vol. 1, p. 37.

294. *Sefer Hasichot 5752*, vol. 1, p. 88.

295. The Talmud, *Menachos* 53b. *Shulchan Aruch Orach Chaim* 46:3. *Shulchan Aruch Harav, Orach Chaim* 46:1.

296. *Torat Menachem 5751*, vol. 1, p. 315. See *Shulchan Aruch Harav, Orach Chaim* 46:1.

A Boy's

Beginnings

The Rebbe wanted milestone events to serve as opportunities to educate a wider audience. When we were living in Norfolk, Virginia, our eldest son turned three years old. As is the Chasidic custom, his hair had not been cut until then, a custom unheard of in the city. His birthday fell on a Sunday and was celebrated privately the previous evening with a *Malave Malka,* a post-Shabbat meal, with family and a few friends.

The next day, the Rebbe's personal chief aide, Rabbi Chaim Mordechai Aizik Hodakov, called and said that the Rebbe had inquired how my son's *opsherenish* would be celebrated.

I responded that it had already been held the previous evening. Rabbi Hodakov hung up after leaving his best wishes. A few hours later, Rabbi Hodakov called again and said that the Rebbe was disappointed because the opportunity to introduce this custom to the Jewish community had been missed.

The Rebbe conveyed the message to me that teachable moments should never be passed up. Even a private occasion can be transformed into a community-wide learning experience. He wanted all such events to become learning experiences and, in the process, to demonstrate to others our pride in adhering to Jewish customs.

First Haircut

The custom is not to cut or trim a boy's hair until he has reached the age of three. The *opsherenish* is an important Jewish custom meant to educate the child to leave his sidelocks, the *peyot,* longer that the rest of his hair. From the time of the haircut, the custom is to make a point of training the child to wear ritual fringes, *tzitzit*, and recite the morning blessings, the grace after meals, and the bedtime Shema prayer.[297]

In addition, while many begin even earlier, the child should cover his head,[298] also while sleeping.[299]

Divine Merit

The *opsherenish* is the time to begin educating the child into holiness. This devotion to education awakens a Divine light from above for the child being educated.[300]

Honey Cake

There is a custom to connect the event marking the first time a child goes to Jewish primary school with honey cake, which is called *lekach*, meaning instruction in Hebrew, and alludes to the verse in Proverbs, "For I give you good instruction," referring to the Torah.[301]

A Visual Reminder

From an early age, a boy should wear *tzitzit*,[302] thus testifying that he is a servant of G-d.[303] Beyond hearing about G-d from his parents, actually seeing the *tzitzit* reminds him – and those who see him wearing them – to fulfill other mitzvahs.[304]

297. *Hayom Yom*, entry for Iyar 4.

298. *Igrot Kodesh,* vol. 9, p. 181.

299. Ibid, vol. 3, p. 397.

300. Ibid, vol. 14, p. 39.

301. *Sichot Kodesh 5752*, vol. 1, p. 344.

302. *Torat Menachem 5748*, vol. 2, p. 421, fn. 27. See *Igrot Kodesh Admor HaRashab*, p. 905.

303. *Likkutei Sichot*, vol. 3, p. 273.

304. *Torat Menachem 5748*, vol. 2, p. 421.

Teen

Idealism

Teenage years are a time of searching for meaning and purpose. These critical years are also a time of self-doubt, inner turmoil and insecurity. Teens are confused by feelings that they don't fully grasp, and they at times mask their fears with bravado or extreme behavior. At the same time, they are idealistic and often impressionable.

The Rebbe saw an underlying purity in their motivations. He believed that teens are seeking real meaning, and are yearning for something truly spiritual, a quest after ultimate truth. He interpreted their rejection of more archaic values as a rejection of hypocrisy, and thus an invitation to the truth of Torah. But he was concerned that their self-doubt often left them impressionable and vulnerable to foreign ideologies. Because of this, the Rebbe encouraged his emissaries to reach out to teens and college students and introduce them to authentic Torah life.

The selections that follow show the Rebbe's concern for the delicate balance that parents and teachers need to tread when interacting with youth. They must be careful not to demand or dictate to their charges, while trying to impact them meaningfully.

The Rebbe wanted to appeal to the intellect of teens

while engaging them emotionally. He cautioned adults to be aware of attitudes that might be masking inner turmoil. Parents and teachers need to be considerate of this, he said, in order to have a calming influence on teens.

As for addressing biological changes and development throughout puberty, the Rebbe did not vary from the approach of traditional Judaism. The discussion of intimate matters should be personalized to the particular character of a young man or woman, and there is not a "one size fits all" approach.

The Rebbe was sensitive to the varying cultural nuances of different Jewish communities and advocated working with, rather than challenging, community standards. Therefore, when reading what follows, one must keep in mind that, in his personal letters, the Rebbe addressed each individual according to their circumstances and needs, and his advice was not always uniform.

Craving Purpose

Many philosophies and ideals, from the extreme left to the extreme right, have resulted in widespread disappointment. This discouragement affects mainly the youth who have not seen life illuminated with the values of the Jewish people, the eternal nation, and they feel a void. Therefore, if ever it was necessary to give meaning to day-to-day life according to Torah and tradition, it is in this generation.

The most undesirable consequences arise when life enters a pattern widely known as "the grey world," and when there is no special movement providing youth the opportunity to reveal their inner strengths of courage and self-sacrifice. How will parents respond when their children will one day ask, "Why were we not given fundamental values that would provide meaning, and encouragement to battle a difficult and conflicted existence?" Parents have the obligation to fill this deficiency in their children's education in accordance with the dictum of the great sage Hillel,[305] "If not now, when?"[306]

PART VI Stages of Education

Discussing Intimate Matters

The sages state, "If there is a concern in the heart [in this case, of the youth], it should be shared and discussed with others."[307] On the other hand, in regard to sensual desires, the sages say, "There is a small organ in a man; when it is satiated, it hungers, and when it is made to hunger, it is satiated."[308]

Therefore, the appropriate solution is for teachers to consult with one another and decide how to proceed regarding a particular student. They should speak to students individually, or at most, small groups of two or three students for whom such a discussion would be suitable, obviously talking with the genders separately.

However, this should not be done in a public manner as is customary in many places. Even then, great deliberation is required in order not to cause others, or oneself, to stumble by violating the prohibition[309] of being enticed into thinking forbidden thoughts and the like.[310]

It is incumbent on the parent to maintain a pleasant relationship with their child, especially in their teenage years when there is naturally more tension. As a person grows and matures, the mind will increasingly prevail, but at a young age, this is not a given.

It is important to emphasize that, at all times and especially nowadays, we must be exceedingly careful about anything related to the nerves of the young generation, considering the state of their mental health.[311]

To combat this, our sages state that there are three categories of people about whom it is said one should embrace with their "right hand," referring to the preferred hand of most people; one of them is a child.[312]

In some cases, it is recommended to consult with a psychologist, since often, and perhaps even in most cases, the behavior is related to nervous tension and a psychologist has the skill to assist significantly.[313]

Proper Tools

We see that many of our young people are confused and lost while searching for truth. Experience has shown that when one conveys something genuine, the youth are eager to listen and take up a challenge, even if it means a complete transformation of their way of life.

However, in order to have a lasting impact, it is not sufficient to give them limited opportunities for Torah learning. They need to be provided with ample opportunity in the form of a Torah-based educational institution with proper, befitting facilities.[314]

Hypocrisy Unwelcome

In this generation, the youth themselves ridicule those who walk a nebulous line, saying that if teachers and educators would themselves believe in what they were teaching, the youth would have more trust and commitment. This is especially so in matters connected to G-d's Torah, as it is self-evident that a man of flesh and blood has no authority to compromise in such matters.[315]

Particular Attention

Young women in general, and particularly during the years of puberty, are more prone to inner turmoil. Therefore, working with them in small groups is praiseworthy. In addition, there are not enough words to describe the merit, and worthiness, of all efforts to improve the environment in which they study.[316]

The Environment

It is essential for teen students, who at this age are very impressionable, to always remain in an appropriate environment.[317]

305. Ethics of Our Fathers 1:14.

306. *Igrot Kodesh*, vol. 22, pp. 189-190.

307. Cf. Proverbs 12:25; The Talmud, *Yoma* 75a.

308. The Talmud, *Sukkah* 52b.

309. See *Shulchan Aruch, Even HaEzer* 23:3; cf. *Tanya* ch. 11.

310. *Likkutei Sichot*, vol. 22, p. 404.

311. *Igrot Kodesh*, vol. 24, p. 18.

312. The Talmud, *Sanhedrin*, 107b.

313. *Igrot Kodesh*, vol. 15, p. 224.

314. *Letters from the Rebbe*, vol. 2, p. 40.

315. *Igrot Kodesh*, vol. 7, p. 239.

316. Ibid, vol. 12, p. 191.

317. Ibid, vol. 9, p. 200.

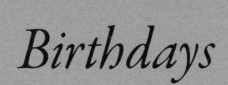

Birthdays

The Rebbe never let an occasion pass quietly. He was a proponent of celebrating milestones and special occasions as a means to help individuals nurture their spiritual selves.

He suggested that everyone mark and celebrate birthdays (and other personal anniversaries), not as an excuse to throw a party, but as an opportunity to chart a better course for the next year. He wanted people to look toward the future rather than dwell on the past.

This was true for children as much as it was for adults. He suggested that children have birthday celebrations during which they make a public resolution concerning their personal and spiritual development.

On infant or toddler birthdays, the Rebbe wanted parents to contemplate their good fortune, and their responsibility to raise children with a focus on spiritual potential rather than just providing for their physical needs.

Even customs regarding minor rites of passage were seen by the Rebbe as opportunities to celebrate their religious meaning and importance. For example, the Rebbe strongly advocated adherence to the Kabbalistic custom to leave a boy's hair uncut until his third birthday, and he would send a congratulatory letter to the parents upon the first hair-cutting.

When it came to celebrations of Bar and Bat Mitzvah, the Rebbe wanted the occasion to retain its essential meaning and be used as an opportunity for spiritual growth.

Communal milestones were deemed important occasions for fostering new activity, which invariably included practical resolutions for a better future.

Joy of Life

While the fetus moves independently, it's still entirely dependent on its mother for sustenance; thus, it is not considered an independent living person until it is born. This is the reason for the joy of a birthday. On this day, each person was given life and the ability to serve G-d through Torah and mitzvahs.[318]

The First Birthday

When a child reaches their first birthday, parents should increase their own daily study of Torah and give additional charity in their child's merit. They should contemplate the great privilege that the Almighty entrusted them to care for a holy soul, and to raise them in the proper G-dly path.[319]

PART VI Stages of Education

Birthday Customs

On one's birthday, a person should spend time focused on the three pillars upon which the world stands: Torah study, prayer, and charity. On this day, they should also make a joyous gathering with their friends.

Additionally, it is a time to make positive resolutions for the following year in matters relating to Torah and mitzvahs. The resolutions should be made in a public forum, which holds more strength than making a resolution alone.[320] This also creates an opportunity for accountability.[321]

The above customs should be emphasized to the youth, for they do everything with enthusiasm, which will excite their younger siblings to celebrate birthdays in a fitting way.

Moreover, when children properly celebrate their birthdays, when it is a parent's birthday, they will make a fuss about the above practices, which will include the parent making good resolutions.

Torah Idea

On a birthday, parents and teachers should encourage and assist the child to speak about a Torah topic.[322]

318. *Likkutei Sichot*, vol. 24, pp. 180.

319. *Torat Menachem 5742*, vol. 4, p. 2190.

320. *Sefer HaMaamarim 5659*, s.v. *Heichaltzu* ch. 10.

321. *Torat Menachem 5748*, vol. 2, p. 461.

322. *Torat Menachem 5750*, vol. 1, p. 162.

Acknowledgements

It is my pleasant duty to acknowledge those who helped bring this project to fruition.

First, many thanks to Rabbi Dovid Zaklikowski who reviewed the manuscript, made many excellent suggestions and essentially ran with it through the production process, I owe him a great dept of gratitude.

To his team at Hasidic Archives, Chana Lewis, Sarah Ogince, Julian Anderson, Shira Yael Klein and Yitzchok Cohen. To Esti Raskin for the art on the cover and throughout the book and Elana Rudick for the cover design.

To Karen Gordon whose original work and research on the Rebbe's chinuch ideas, relevant writings and talks, inspired this effort. To Uriella Sagiv, a talented editor for her excellent work.

Last but surely not least, to my wife of more than half a century, Esther, for her perseverance and encouragement throughout our journey through life together.

Dedicated to My Mother

As this was being written, my mother, Sarah Kaplan, of blessed memory, passed away. She was a remarkable woman, intelligent and well-educated, refined, and cultured, yet modest and understated. She grew up in the agnostic Soviet Union, in a home where Torah teachings were pre-eminent in spite of brutal, anti-religious persecution. Her father was ultimately arrested for his dedication to maintaining and strengthening Jewish life. Tortured and sent to a labor camp in Siberia, he perished under the harshest conditions during his first winter there.

Doubly orphaned in her teens, my mother suffered poverty and oppression but remained steadfast in her observance of Judaism under the severest conditions. Narrowly escaping German extermination, she eventually made her way to the West where she raised a Chasidic family and by the grace of Almighty G-d lived a long and productive life, long enough to see her great, great grandchildren.

This volume is dedicated to her, for without her gentle guidance I would not be me.